"★ ★ ★ ★ ★ Thrillingly modern and moving. *Dear Evan Hansen* takes on challenging subjects—death, grief, class, mental illness, social media, social anxiety—with unapologetic trust in the power of contemporary pop music to tell complex stories onstage. It must be seen to be believed."

—ADAM FELDMAN, *TIME OUT NEW YORK*

"Extraordinary. A fresh, intricately plotted book by Steven Levenson, and a banquet of ballads of anguish and confusion, which somehow avoid sentimental exploitation, by Pasek and Paul. It is the heart of a superbly crafted and performed show that is unafraid of complexity and ambiguity. *Dear Evan Hansen* is the first great American musical about social media—a democratizer, comforter, amoral facilitator of witch hunts and general pox Americana that has upended everything from family mealtime to who gets to occupy the Oval Office. It is a show that seems to understand in a way that others do not, have not, might not soon again." **—CHRIS JONES, *CHICAGO TRIBUNE***

"*Dear Evan Hansen* is a heart-scorching musical. It is cathartic and real and very funny. This musical reaches a generation that can seem jaded or desensitized, having come of age with access to the entire world's pain and tribulations in the palm of their hand."

—SUSANNA SCHROBSDORFF, *TIME MAGAZINE*

"A dazzlingly reminder of the power of live theater."

—JOE DZIEMIANOWICZ, *DAILY NEWS*

"A modern masterwork. *Dear Evan Hansen* is absorbing, wrenching, heartbreaking, and at the same time exhilarating. This is a show that captures your attention immediately, enchants you with its characters and songs, pulls you through emotional turbulence, and leaves you cheering and wanting to go back for more."

—STEVEN SUSKIN, *HUFFINGTON POST*

"Watching *Dear Evan Hansen* is like falling down a rabbit hole that leads back to high school. Steven Levenson's book for this bittersweet musical captures both the humor and the pathos of a hopeless misfit who achieves popularity through no fault of his own. And the introspective, gentle score by Benj Pasek and Justin Paul becomes the language of Evan's troubled thoughts and unspoken yearnings. The lyrics and score seamlessly merge with the dialogue of Levenson's book. In song after song, the lyrics go beyond the spoken thought and reach for the unspoken feelings hiding behind the words without a hint of sentimentality."

—MARILYN STASIO, *VARIETY*

"Stunning and original and profound. Songwriters Pasek and Paul have written one of Broadway's most exciting and catchy new scores. Each tune sounds fresh and authentic to its character. Steven Levenson has done wonders crafting a story filled with characters and dialogue that expertly avoid the cliché. Levenson finds surprises along the way while never failing to explore his characters' often-conflicting emotions. Bravo!"

—DAVE QUINN, NBC4

"The cacophonous echo chamber of social media, with all its attendant rewards and perils of instant recognition or scathing judgment, is given forceful shape in the original *Dear Evan Hansen*, a musical of piercing intimacy. It is a smart, soulful depiction of teen solitude graced by both gentle humor and raw feeling. The score beautifully captures the peaks and valleys of adolescence, in the thoughtful lyrics and in the music, and Steven Levenson matches the musical components beat for beat in his terrific book."   **—DAVID ROONEY, *HOLLYWOOD REPORTER***

"*Dear Evan Hansen* is an important (and seriously delightful) addition to the twenty-first-century musical. It is superb— original, sensitive, provocative, endearing. Everyone is a fully developed person in Steven Levenson's smart book, and the clever, sympathetic songs by Benj Pasek and Justin Paul have a singer/songwriter pop intimacy that challenges expansive vocal ranges without seeming to show off."   **—LINDA WINER,** *NEWSDAY*

"That rare show that connects and enlightens all of us. Pasek and Paul's score, so seamlessly woven into the story line, captures character nuances with the emotional eloquence of our finest dramatic plays, inducing tears and laughter in equal measure."

—ROMA TORRE, NY1

"Devastatingly powerful. The musical boasts a darkly textured and deeply nuanced book by Steven Levenson and provocative songs by Benj Pasek and Justin Paul that are drenched in feeling and fearless commitment. It never sentimentalizes its subject, but feels constantly truthful."

—MARK SHENTON, *STAGE* **(LONDON)**

"Leaving a new musical with a great song or two running through your head is a rare but exciting thing. Leaving with about ten great songs running through your head is pretty much unheard of. But that's the power of *Dear Evan Hansen.* It's not simply that the songs are tuneful. It's that they have a way of instantly piercing your heart and burrowing into your consciousness, while also illuminating character and propelling the plot (no small achievement!). Credit librettist Steven Levenson for creating such a believable young character in Evan, from the anxiety meds to the self-deprecating dialogue. And don't be surprised if, to one degree or another, you see yourself in Evan. "On the outside always lookin' in / Will I ever be more than I've always been?" he sings in the show-stopping "Waving Through a Window." It's Evan's confessional, but it might as well be an anthem for outcasts, loners, and misfits everywhere."

—MELISSA ROSE BERNARDO, *ENTERTAINMENT WEEKLY*

DEAR
EVAN
HANSEN

DEAR EVAN HANSEN

BOOK BY
STEVEN LEVENSON

MUSIC AND LYRICS BY
BENJ PASEK & **JUSTIN PAUL**

THEATRE COMMUNICATIONS GROUP
NEW YORK
2017

Dear Evan Hansen is published by Theatre Communications Group, Inc.,
520 Eighth Avenue, 24th Floor, New York, NY 10018-4156

The publication of *Dear Evan Hansen* by Steven Levenson, Benj Pasek & Justin
Paul, through TCG's Book Program, is made possible in part by the New York
State Council on the Arts with the support of Governor Andrew Cuomo and
the New York State Legislature.

TCG books are exclusively distributed to the book trade by Consortium Book
Sales and Distribution.

ISBN 978-1-55936-560-4 (paperback) / ISBN 978-1-55936-880-3 (ebook)

A catalog record for this book is available from the Library of Congress.

Book design and composition by Lisa Govan
Watercolor by Emily Rebholz

First Edition, April 2017
Fourth Printing, August 2017

To Whitney and Astrid.
–STEVEN

To Mary, Annie, Maceo, and the Llanerch Diner.
–BENJ

To Asher, Emerson, Mom, Dad, and Tyler.
For always believing.
–JUSTIN

CONTENTS

ACKNOWLEDGMENTS

So many people have contributed to the development of *Dear Evan Hansen*, but we owe a special debt of gratitude to David Berlin, John Buzzetti, Adrienne Campbell-Holt, John Dossett, Clive Goodwin, David Korins, Alex Lacamoire, LP3, Joe Machota, Michael McGoff, Danny Mefford, Alexis Molnar, Peter Nigrini, Wendy Orshan, Emily Rebholz, Judy Schoenfeld, Nevin Steinberg, Jack Viertel, Japhy Weideman, and Jeffrey M. Wilson, as well as Arena Stage, Second Stage Theatre, and the Shubert Organization. We will be forever grateful to the tremendous ensemble of actors that make up the company of *Dear Evan Hansen*—Laura Dreyfuss, Mike Faist, Rachel Bay Jones, Kristolyn Lloyd, Michael Park, Ben Platt, Will Roland, and Jennifer Laura Thompson—all of whom have devoted every ounce of themselves to bringing these characters and this world to life, always with courage, humor, and a boundless generosity of spirit. Special thanks to Michael Greif, whose artistry and intellect are only matched by the capaciousness of his vision and the extraordinary depths of his empathy. Finally, none of this would have been possible without the unwavering devotion of Stacey Mindich, who believed in this musical even when we didn't, and who urged us, always, to keep going.

FOREWORD

By James Lapine

How a musical is made is a bit of a mystery, even to those of us who write them.

At the end of the day, creating a musical is a marriage of writers who come together to speak with one voice, to marry words to music. In a successful musical there is a seamless flow where characters sing effortlessly and the story carries you along in such a way that you often don't make the distinction between dialogue and song. To have any hope of succeeding, the collaborators first have to choose a story with characters that by their very nature have to express themselves in song.

The young creators of the extraordinary *Dear Evan Hansen*—book writer Steven Levenson and composer/lyricists Benj Pasek and Justin Paul—have not only met this challenge but have done so from an original idea with important overtones. For those of you who have seen the show, or maybe are only familiar with it from the cast recording, to now read *Dear Evan Hansen* is a wonderful guide to how a musical is constructed and an opportunity to discover how dialogue and lyrics live and breathe independent of music. And for those of you who know nothing about this piece, this book in and of itself will still be a very satisfying read.

The eloquence and economy of the opening stage direction gives us a hint of this show's originality. It does not begin with the traditional "opening number" but rather a monologue in the form of a letter. What follows is a masterful structure— both in storytelling and dramatic momentum, and in the dance between song and dialogue—that brings us a story that manages to be both funny and deeply moving. Reading *Dear Evan Hansen* without the support of music—that ineffable force that speaks more to our heart than our head—one can still marvel at the musicality of the dialogue and lyrics which stand impressively on their own terms.

We laugh when Jared says: "Literally, nothing I tell my parents is true and they have no idea." Those of us of a certain age come to learn that our parents knew more about our youthful lies than they ever let on; and as we matured we began to discover and sometimes painfully face our parents' lies as well. The search for "truth" and "self" lies at the center of *Dear Evan Hansen*. The story of Connor's death is the common denominator that brings these seven characters together with Evan at the center. "Everybody needed [this story] for something." A central lie sends these characters on their journey together.

Dear Evan Hansen is set in our current world of "fake news," "alternative facts," and faceless and unaccountable internet/ Twitter chatter. With laser focus and simplicity, the authors bring clarity to the basic human impulse to be heard and seen, to be understood, and, ultimately, to love and be loved. The layers of this inspired show will subtly unveil themselves when you read this work:

"You will be found . . ."

"What if ev'ryone knew? / Would they like what they saw?"

"You think you're going to turn around all of a sudden and start telling everyone the truth? You can't even tell yourself the truth."

Dear Evan Hansen lodges in your head long after you've seen it or heard it or read it. It feels like a pure expression from young writers at a crossroad of coming to terms with who they are and what they want to say about the world. Its honesty and truths haunt and ultimately open us up to ask the same question, no matter what our age or crossroad: What are the lies we tell ourselves?

New York City
March 21, 2017

JAMES LAPINE is a playwright, librettist, screenwriter, stage director, and filmmaker. He was awarded the Pulitzer Prize in Drama, with Stephen Sondheim, for *Sunday in the Park with George*, and received the Tony Award for Best Book of a Musical for *Into the Woods*, *Falsettos*, and *Passion*.

DEAR EVAN HANSEN

PRODUCTION HISTORY

Dear Evan Hansen had its world premiere at Arena Stage (Molly Smith, Artistic Director; Edgar Dobie, Executive Director) in Washington, DC, on July 30, 2015. It was directed by Michael Greif. The scenic design was by David Korins, the costume design was by Emily Rebholz, the lighting design was by Japhy Weideman, the sound design was by Clive Goodwin, the projection design was by Peter Nigrini; the music director was Ben Cohn, the music supervisor and orchestrator was Alex Lacamoire, the choreographer was Danny Mefford, and the production stage manager was Judith Schoenfeld. The cast was:

EVAN HANSEN	Ben Platt
HEIDI HANSEN	Rachel Bay Jones
ZOE MURPHY	Laura Dreyfuss
CONNOR MURPHY	Mike Faist
CYNTHIA MURPHY	Jennifer Laura Thompson
LARRY MURPHY	Michael Park
JARED KLEINMAN	Will Roland
ALANA BECK	Alexis Molnar

Dear Evan Hansen had its New York premiere at Second Stage Theatre (Carole Rothman, Artistic Director; Casey Reitz, Executive Director) on May 1, 2016. The cast and creative team remained the same as the Arena Stage production, except the sound design was by Nevin Steinberg, and:

LARRY MURPHY	John Dossett
ALANA BECK	Kristolyn Lloyd

Dear Evan Hansen opened on Broadway at The Music Box Theatre on December 4, 2016. The producers were Stacey Mindich, Mickey Liddell, Hunter Arnold, Caiola Productions, Double Gemini Productions, Fakston Productions, Roy Furman, Harris Karma Productions, On Your Marks Group, Darren Bagert, Roger & William Berlind, Bob Boyett, Colin Callender, Caitlin Clements, Freddy DeMann, Dante Di Loreto, Bonnie & Kenneth Feld, FickStern Productions, Eric & Marsi Gardiner, Robert Greenblatt, Jere Harris and Darren DeVerna, The Jorn Gore Organization, Mike Kriak, Arielle Tepper Madover, David Mirvish, Eva Price, Zeilinger Productions, Adam Zotovich, Ambassador Theatre Group, Independent Presenters Network, and the Shubert Organization. The executive producers were Wendy Orshan and Jeffrey M. Wilson. The cast and creative team remained the same as the Second Stage Theatre production, except wigs and hair were designed by David Brian Brown, and:

LARRY MURPHY	Michael Park

CHARACTERS

EVAN HANSEN, seventeen
HEIDI HANSEN, Evan's mother, forties
ZOE MURPHY, sixteen
CONNOR MURPHY, Zoe's brother, seventeen
CYNTHIA MURPHY, Connor and Zoe's mother, forties
LARRY MURPHY, Connor and Zoe's father, forties
JARED KLEINMAN, seventeen
ALANA BECK, seventeen

SET

A blank, empty space, filled with screens.

NOTE

A forward slash " / " indicates a point of overlapping dialogue.

SONGS

Act One

Anybody Have a Map?	*Heidi, Cynthia*
Waving Through a Window	*Evan, Company*
For Forever	*Evan*
Sincerely, Me	*Connor, Evan, Jared*
Requiem	*Zoe, Cynthia, Larry*
If I Could Tell Her	*Evan, Zoe*
Disappear	*Connor, Evan, Alana, Jared, Cynthia, Larry, Zoe*
You Will Be Found	*Evan, Virtual Community, Company*

Act Two

Sincerely, Me (Reprise)	*Connor, Jared*
To Break in a Glove	*Larry, Evan*
Only Us	*Zoe, Evan*
Good for You	*Heidi, Alana, Jared, Evan*
You Will Be Found (Reprise)	*Alana, Jared, Virtual Community*
Words Fail	*Evan*
So Big/So Small	*Heidi*
Finale	*Company*

ACT ONE

ONE

A quiet buzzing begins to sound just at the edge of our awareness, an indistinct murmuring of voices, as the house lights slowly fade.

The murmuring builds, growing louder and louder, voices piling on top of one another.

Millions of fragments of emails, status updates, cat videos, dessert recipes, revenge porn—the music of the spheres.

Of a sort.

Suddenly, sharply, nothing.

Silence.

Then, in the darkness, a laptop snaps open.

The gauzy white glow of the screen illuminates the face of Evan Hansen, sitting at a desk with a hard cast on his left arm, alone.

He begins to type.

EVAN: Dear Evan Hansen:

Today is going to be an amazing day, and here's why. Because today, all you have to do is just be yourself.

(Beat.)

But also confident. That's important. And interesting. Easy to talk to. Approachable. But mostly be yourself. That's the big, that's number one. Be yourself. Be true to yourself.

(Beat.)

Also, though, don't worry about whether your hands are going to get sweaty for no reason and you can't make it stop no matter what you do, because they're not going to get sweaty, so I don't even know why you're bringing it up, because it's not going to happen, because you're just, all you have to do is be yourself.

(Beat.)

I'm not even going to worry about it, though, because seriously it's not like, it's not going to be like that time you had the perfect chance to introduce yourself to Zoe Murphy at the jazz band concert last year, when you waited afterward to talk to her and tell her how good she was, and you were going to pretend to be super casual like you didn't even know her name, like she would introduce herself and you'd be like, "Wait, I'm sorry, I didn't hear you. Chloe, you said your name was Chloe?" And she'd be, like, "No, it's Zoe, I said, Zoe," and you'd be, like, "Oh, see, I thought you said Chloe because I don't even, I'm very busy with other stuff right now is the thing." But then you didn't even end up saying anything to her anyway, because you were scared your hands were sweaty which they weren't that sweaty until you started worrying that they were sweaty, which made them sweaty, so you put them under the hand dryer in the bathroom, but then they were still sweaty, they were just very warm now, as well.

(Lights shift and Heidi Hansen stands there, holding a twenty-dollar bill.)

HEIDI: So you just decided not to eat last night?

(Evan quickly shuts his laptop.)

EVAN: Oh, I'm, um, I wasn't hungry . . .

HEIDI: You're a senior in high school, Evan. You need to be able to order dinner for yourself if I'm at work. You can do it all online now. You don't have to talk to anyone on the phone. I know you don't like the phone.

EVAN: Okay, but see, that's not true actually. You have to talk to the delivery person when they come to the door. Then they have to make change. You have to stand there while it's silent and they're counting the change and . . .

HEIDI: This is what you're supposed to be working on, Evan. With Dr. Sherman? Talking to people. Engaging with people. Not running away from people.

EVAN: You're right. I'm going to be a lot better.

HEIDI *(Trying to put a positive spin on it)*: No, I know. I know you are. And that's why I made you an appointment with Dr. Sherman for this afternoon. I'll pick you up right after school.

EVAN: I already have an appointment next week.

HEIDI: And I thought maybe you could use something a little sooner. Have you been writing those letters he wants you to do? The letters to yourself? The pep talks? "Dear Evan

Hansen. This is going to be a good day and here's why."
Have you been doing those?

EVAN: I started writing one. I'll finish it at school.

HEIDI: Those letters are important, honey. They're going to
help you build your confidence. Seize the day.

EVAN *(Dubious)*: I guess.

HEIDI: I don't want another year of you sitting at home on your
computer every Friday night, telling me you have no friends.

(Beat.)

EVAN: Neither do I.

ANYBODY HAVE A MAP?

HEIDI:

Can we try to have an optimistic outlook?

Huh?

Can we buck up just enough
To see . . . the world won't fall apart?
Maybe this year we decide
We're not giving up before we've tried
This year, we make a new start

Hey, I know—you can go around today and ask the other
kids to sign your cast, how about that? That would be the
perfect icebreaker, wouldn't it?

EVAN: Perfect.

HEIDI: I'm proud of you already.

EVAN: Oh. Good.

(Heidi exits the room, stands in the hall, realizing that this inter-action has been an utter failure, as Evan packs up for school.)

HEIDI:
> *Another stellar conversation for the scrapbook*
> *Another stumble as I'm reaching for*
> *The right thing to say*
> *Well, I'm kinda comin' up empty*
> *Can't find my way to you*
>
> *Does anybody have a map?*
> *Anybody maybe happen to know how the hell to do this?*
> *I dunno if you can tell*
> *But this is me just pretending to know*
>
> *So where's the map?*
> *I need a clue*
> *'Cause the scary truth is*
> *I'm flyin' blind*
> *And I'm making this up as I go*

(Lights shift to find the Murphys at the kitchen table. Zoe Murphy sits, eating cereal, leafing through a book. Larry Murphy, on his phone, scrolls through emails. Connor Murphy stares blankly into his cereal bowl. Cynthia Murphy stands, fussing over everything—pouring orange juice, topping off coffee, clearing finished dishes.)

CYNTHIA: It's your senior year, Connor. You are not missing the first day.

CONNOR: I already said I'd go tomorrow. I'm trying to find a compromise here.

CYNTHIA *(Turns to Larry)*: Are you going to get involved here or are you too busy on your email, Larry?

LARRY: You have to go to school, Connor.

CYNTHIA: That's all you're going to say?

LARRY: What do you want me to say? He doesn't listen. Look at him. He's not listening. He's probably high.

ZOE: He's definitely high.

CONNOR *(To Zoe)*: Fuck you.

ZOE: Fuck you.

CYNTHIA *(Admonishing Zoe)*: I don't need you picking at your brother right now. That is not constructive.

ZOE: Are you kidding?

CYNTHIA: Besides, he is not high.

(Cynthia looks to Connor to confirm this.
He does not.
She sighs.)

I do not want you going to school high, Connor. We have talked about this.

CONNOR: Perfect. So then I won't go. Thanks, Mom.

(Connor leaves.
Cynthia begins clearing the dishes, lost in her own thoughts.)

CYNTHIA:

> *Another masterful attempt ends with disaster*

(Larry, looking at his phone, shakes his head.)

LARRY: Interstate's already jammed.

CYNTHIA:

> *Pour another cup of coffee*
> *And watch it all crash and burn*

(Zoe goes to pour herself more milk, shakes the carton, annoyed.)

ZOE: Connor finished the milk.

CYNTHIA:

> *It's a puzzle, it's a maze*
> *I try to steer through it a million ways*
> *But each day's another wrong turn*

(Larry stands, offering Cynthia a perfunctory spousal peck.)

LARRY: I better head out.
ZOE: If Connor's not ready, I'm leaving without him . . .

(She and Larry exit.)

CYNTHIA:

Does anybody	HEIDI:
Have a map?	*Anybody have a map*
Anybody maybe happen	*Or happen*
To know how the hell	*To know how the hell*
To do this?	*To do this?*
I dunno if you can tell	*I dunno if you can tell*
But this is me just	*But this is me just*
Pretending to know	*Pretending to know*

(Evan and Connor appear in separate pools of light, just outside the school doors, fiddling with shirt collars, smoothing hair, and—for Evan—checking palms for signs of dampness, as the two young men anxiously prepare to face the day.)

HEIDI:

> *So where's the map?*

CYNTHIA:

   I need a clue

HEIDI/CYNTHIA:

   'Cause the scary truth is

CYNTHIA:

I'm flyin' blind

                HEIDI:

                I'm flyin' blind

I'm flyin' blind

                I'm flyin'

I'm flyin' blind   *I'm flyin' blind*

And I'm making this up   *And I'm making this up*

As I go   *As I go*

As I go   *As I go*

(*As Cynthia and Heidi exit, the buzz of a school bell.
Lights shift, finding Evan standing in a school hallway.
Alana Beck enters, a certain barely concealed desperation in the
eagerness with which she approaches Evan, in her almost too-
wide smile.*)

ALANA: Hey. How was your summer?

(*Evan looks around, not sure if she's speaking to someone else.*)

EVAN: My . . . ?

ALANA: Mine was productive. I did three internships and ninety hours of community service. I know: wow.

EVAN: Yeah. That's, wow. / That's really impressive.

ALANA: / Even though I was so busy, I still made some great friends. Or, well, acquaintances, more like.

EVAN *(Gathering his courage)*: Do you want to maybe . . . I don't know what you're, um . . . do you want to sign my cast?

ALANA: Oh my God. What happened to your arm?

EVAN: Oh. Well. I broke it. I was climbing a tree . . .

ALANA *(Not listening at all)*: Oh really? My grandma broke her hip getting into the bathtub in July. That was the beginning of the end, the doctors said. Because then she died.

(Evan has no idea how to respond to this.
Alana plasters on a glowing smile.)

Happy first day.

(Alana exits as Jared Kleinman approaches Evan with the kind of practiced swagger only the deeply insecure can truly pull off.)

JARED: Is it weird to be the first person in history to break their arm from jerking off too much or do you consider that an honor?

EVAN: Wait. What? I didn't, I wasn't . . . doing that.

JARED: Paint me the picture: you're in your bedroom, you've got Zoe Murphy's Instagram up on your weird, off-brand cell phone . . .

EVAN: That's not what happened. Obviously. I was, um, well I was climbing a tree and I fell.

JARED: You fell out of a tree? What are you, like, an acorn?

EVAN: Well, I was, I don't know if you know this, but I worked this summer as an apprentice park ranger at Ellison State Park. I'm sort of a tree expert now. Not to brag, but . . .

(Jared says nothing.)

Anyway. I tried to climb this forty-foot-tall oak tree.

JARED: And then you fell . . . ?

EVAN: Well, except it's a funny story, because there was this solid ten minutes after I fell, when I just lay there on the ground waiting for someone to come get me. Any second now, I kept saying to myself. Any second now, here they come.

JARED: Did they?

EVAN: No. Nobody came. That's the, that's what's funny.

JARED: Jesus Christ . . .

EVAN: How was, what did you do for the, you had a good summer?

JARED: Well, my bunk dominated in capture the flag and I got to second-base-below-the-bra with this girl from Israel who's going to like be in the army . . . so, yeah, hopefully that answers your question.

(Jared turns to go.)

EVAN: Do you want to sign my cast?

JARED: Why are you asking me?

EVAN: Well, just, I thought, because we're friends.

JARED: We're family friends. That's like a whole different thing and you know it.

(He punches Evan in the arm.)

Hey. Tell your mom to tell my mom I was nice to you or else my parents won't pay for my car insurance.

EVAN: I will.

(Connor crosses.)

JARED: Hey, Connor. I'm loving the new hair length. Very school shooter chic.

(Connor stops, casts a withering glance at him.)

I was kidding. It was a joke.

CONNOR *(Deadpan)*: Yeah, no, it was funny. I'm laughing. Can't you tell? Am I not laughing hard enough for you?

JARED *(Laughs nervously, bravado gone)*: You're such a freak.

(Jared, laughing, nervously exits.
Connor turns to Evan.
Evan laughs, uncomfortable.)

CONNOR: What the fuck are you laughing at?

EVAN: What?

CONNOR: Stop fucking laughing at me.

EVAN: I'm not.

CONNOR: You think I'm a freak?

EVAN: No. I don't—

CONNOR: I'm not the freak.

EVAN: But I wasn't—

CONNOR: You're the fucking freak.

(Connor shoves him to the ground as he storms away.
Slowly, Evan stands.)

WAVING THROUGH A WINDOW

EVAN:

> *I've learned to slam on the brake*
> *Before I even turn the key*
> *Before I make the mistake*
> *Before I lead with the worst of me*

EVAN *(con't):*

> *Give them no reason to stare*
> *No slippin' up if you slip away*
> *So I got nothin' to share*
> *No, I got nothin' to say*
>
> *Step out, step outta the sun*
> *If you keep gettin' burned*
> *Step out, step outta the sun*
> *Because you've learned, because you've learned*
>
> *On the outside always lookin' in*
> *Will I ever be more than I've always been?*
> *'Cause I'm tap-tap-tappin' on the glass*
> *Waving through a window*
>
> *I try to speak but nobody can hear*
> *So I wait around for an answer to appear*
> *While I'm watch-watch-watchin' people pass*
> *Waving through a window*
> *Oh*
> *Can anybody see?*
> *Is anybody waving back at me?*

(Lights shift and Zoe enters.)

ZOE: Hey. I'm sorry about my brother. I saw him push you. He's a psychopath. Evan, right?

EVAN: Evan?

ZOE: That's your name . . . ?

EVAN: Oh. Yes. Evan. It's Evan. Sorry.

ZOE: Why are you sorry?

EVAN: Well, just because you said, Evan, and then I said, I repeated it, which is, that's so annoying when people do that.

ZOE: I'm Zoe.

EVAN: No, I know.

ZOE: You know?

EVAN: No, just, I've seen you play guitar in jazz band. I love jazz band. I love jazz. Not all jazz. But definitely jazz band jazz. That's so weird, I'm sorry.

ZOE: You apologize a lot.

EVAN: I'm sorry.

(He catches himself.)

Or. I mean. You know what I mean.

ZOE: Well, / I'll talk to you later.

EVAN: / You don't want to sign my . . . ?

ZOE: What?

EVAN *(Instantly regretting his decision)*: What? What did you say?

ZOE: I didn't say anything. You said something.

EVAN: No. Me? No way. José.

ZOE: Um. Okay . . . José.

(Zoe exits.)

EVAN:

We start with stars in our eyes
We start believin' that we belong
But ev'ry sun doesn't rise
And no one tells you where you went wrong

Step out, step outta the sun
If you keep gettin' burned
Step out, step outta the sun
Because you've learned, because you've learned

On the outside always lookin' in
Will I ever be more than I've always been?

EVAN *(con't)*:

> *'Cause I'm tap-tap-tappin' on the glass*
> *Waving through a window*
>
> *I try to speak but nobody can hear*
> *So I wait around for an answer to appear*
> *While I'm watch-watch-watchin' people pass*
> *Waving through a window*
> *Oh*
> *Can anybody see?*
> *Is anybody waving . . . ?*
>
> *When you're fallin' in a forest*
> *And there's nobody around*
> *Do you ever really crash*
> *Or even make a sound?*
>
> *When you're fallin' in a forest*
> *And there's nobody around*
> *Do you ever really crash*
> *Or even make a sound?*
>
> *When you're fallin' in a forest*
> *And there's nobody around*
> *Do you ever really crash*
> *Or even make a sound?*

	COMPANY:
When you're fallin' in a forest	*Ah*
And there's nobody around	
Do you ever really crash	*Ah*
Or even make a sound?	
Did I even make a sound?	*Oh*

Did I even make a sound?
It's like I never made a sound   *Oh*
Will I ever make a sound?   *Oh*

On the outside   *Oh*
Always lookin' in
Will I ever be more
Than I've always been?
'Cause I'm tap-tap-tappin'   *Oh*
On the glass
Waving through a window   *Oh*

I try to speak   *Oh*
But nobody can hear
So I wait around
For an answer to appear
While I'm watch-watch-watchin'   *Oh*
People pass
Waving through a window   *Oh*
Oh
Can anybody see?
Is anybody waving . . .
Back at me?
        Oh
Is anybody waving?   *Oh*
Waving
Waving   *Oh*
Oh   *Oh*
Oh oh oh

TWO

Heidi, in her nurse's scrubs, on her cell phone, a bit harried, an eye on the clock.

Evan, at school, on his phone.

HEIDI: Shit, honey. I know I was supposed to pick you up for your appointment. I'm stuck at work. Erica called in with the flu and I'm the only other nurse's aide on today, so I volunteered to pick up her shift . . .

(Evan is used to this, almost expected it.)

EVAN: It's fine.

HEIDI: It's just, they announced more budget cuts this morning, so anything I can do to show that I'm, you know, a team player . . .

EVAN: It's fine. I'll take the bus.

HEIDI *(Relieved)*: Perfect. That's perfect. Oh and I'm going straight from here to class, so I won't be home until late, so please eat something. We've got those Trader Joe's dumplings in the freezer . . .

EVAN: Maybe.

HEIDI: Did you write one of those letters yet? Dr. Sherman's expecting you to have one. "Dear Evan Hansen. This is going to be a good day and here's why"?

EVAN *(Lying)*: Yeah, no, I already finished it. I'm in the computer lab right now, printing it out.

HEIDI: I hope it was a good day, sweetheart.

EVAN: It was . . . yeah, it was really great.

HEIDI: Great. That's great. I hope it's the beginning of a great year. I think we both could use one of those, huh? Shit. I have to run. Bye. I love you.

(Heidi hangs up and goes.)

EVAN: Bye.

(A long moment alone.
Evan opens his laptop and begins to compose his letter.)

Dear Evan Hansen:

It turns out, this wasn't an amazing day after all. This isn't going to be an amazing week or an amazing year. Because . . . why would it be?

Oh I know. Because there's Zoe. And all my hope is pinned on Zoe. Who I don't even know and who doesn't know me. But maybe if I did. Maybe if I could just talk to her, then maybe . . . maybe nothing would be different at all.

I wish that everything was different. I wish that I was a part of . . . something. I wish that anything I said . . . mattered, to anyone. I mean, face it: would anybody even notice if I disappeared tomorrow?

Sincerely, your best and most dearest friend,

Me.

WAVING THROUGH A WINDOW (REPRISE)

EVAN:

*When you're fallin' in a forest
And there's nobody around
Do you ever really crash
Or even make a sound?*

*When you're fallin' in a forest
And there's nobody around
Do you ever really crash
Or even make a—*

(Connor enters, holding a piece of paper.)

CONNOR: So. What happened to your arm?

EVAN: Oh, I um, I fell out of a tree actually.

CONNOR *(Can't help but laugh)*: You fell out of a tree? That is just the saddest fucking thing I've ever heard. Oh my God.

(Evan tries to laugh along.)

EVAN: I know.

CONNOR *(Noticing)*: No one's signed your cast.

EVAN: No, I know.

CONNOR: I'll sign it.

EVAN: Oh. Um . . . you don't have to.

CONNOR: Do you have a Sharpie?

(Beat.
Evan reluctantly pulls out a Sharpie, hands it to Connor.
Evan watches in dismay as Connor signs his name in an outsized
scrawl, covering an entire side of the cast.)

EVAN: Oh. Great. Thanks.

CONNOR: Now we can both pretend that we have friends.

EVAN: Good point.

(Evan takes the marker, turns to go.
Connor holds out the piece of paper.)

CONNOR: Is this yours? I found it on the printer. "Dear Evan
Hansen." That's your name, right?

(Evan feels a surge of fear.)

EVAN: Oh that's just a stupid, it's a paper I had to write for a, um,
for an assignment . . .

(Connor looks down at the paper.)

CONNOR: "Because there's Zoe." *(Realizing)* Is this about my *sister*?

(Connor's mood shifts suddenly, abruptly.)

EVAN: No. Not at all.

CONNOR: You wrote this because you knew that I would find it.

EVAN: What?

CONNOR: You saw that I was the only other person in the computer lab, so you wrote this and you printed it out, so that I would find it.

EVAN: Why / would I do that?

CONNOR: / So I would read some creepy shit you wrote about my sister, and freak out, right? And then you can tell everyone that I'm crazy, right?

EVAN: No. Wait. I don't even, what?

CONNOR: Fuck you.

(He exits with the letter, as Evan calls after him.)

EVAN: But I really, I need that back. Please. Can you just, can you please give it back?

THREE

Evan and Jared, online.

JARED: A letter to yourself? What the crap does that even mean? It's, like, some kind of sex thing?

EVAN: No, it's not a sex thing. It's . . . it was an assignment.

JARED: Why are you talking to me about this?

EVAN: I didn't know who else to talk to. You're my only . . . family friend.

JARED *(Too pathetic to even engage)*: Oh my God.

EVAN: I don't know what to do. He stole the letter from me three days ago, and then he just, he hasn't been at school since.

JARED: That does not bode well for you.

EVAN: What is he going to do with it?

JARED: Who knows? Connor Murphy is batshit out of his mind. Do you remember when he threw a printer at Mrs. G. in second grade, because he didn't get to be line leader that day?

EVAN: Do you think he's going to show the letter to other people?

JARED *(Obviously)*: He's going to ruin your life with it. For sure. I mean, I would.

(Lights out on Evan and Jared as Alana appears alone, scanning her phone for emails, texts, anything, all traces of her typical studied cheeriness gone entirely.)

WAVING THROUGH A WINDOW (REPRISE # 2)

ALANA:

> *On the outside always lookin' in*
> *Will I ever be more than I've always been?*
> *'Cause I'm tap-tap-tappin' on the glass*
> *Waving through a window*

FOUR

The principal's office. Evan stands, confused.
    Cynthia Murphy and Larry Murphy sit.
    Larry is stiff and sober, coiled fury just beneath the surface.
    Cynthia is shattered, reeling.
    They both look exhausted.
    Evan looks petrified.

EVAN: Good morning. Is Mr. Howard . . . ?

(They look at him, uncomprehending.)

I just, sorry, they said on the loudspeaker for me to go to the principal's office . . .

(Larry suddenly realizes what he means.)

LARRY: Mr. Howard is, uh, he stepped out.

EVAN: Oh.

LARRY: We wanted to speak with you in private. If you'd like to maybe . . .

(Larry gestures to a chair, and Evan slowly sits.)

We're, uh . . . we're Connor's parents.

EVAN: Oh.

(Cynthia reaches into her purse and pulls out a folded piece of paper. She holds it lovingly, almost cradling it.)

LARRY: Why don't you go ahead, honey, and . . . ?

CYNTHIA: I'm going as fast as I can.

LARRY: That's not what I said, is it?

(A terrible pause.
Cynthia holds the letter out to Evan, her voice unsteady.)

CYNTHIA: This is . . . Connor . . . he wanted you to have this.

(Evan takes it, his face darkening.)

LARRY: We didn't . . . we'd never heard your name before, Connor never . . . but then we saw . . . "Dear Evan Hansen."

EVAN: He, um, he gave this to you?

LARRY: We didn't know that you two were friends.

EVAN: Friends?

LARRY: We didn't think that Connor had *any* friends. And then we see this note and it's, this seems to suggest pretty clearly that you and Connor were, or at least for Connor, he thought of you as . . .

(He points to the letter.)

I mean, it's right there. "Dear Evan Hansen." It's addressed to you. He wrote it to you.

EVAN *(Realizing)*: You think this is, you think that Connor wrote this to me.

CYNTHIA: These are the words he wanted to share with you.

LARRY: His last words.

CYNTHIA: This is what he wanted you to have.

EVAN: I'm sorry. What do you mean, last words?

(Cynthia and Larry share a look.
A long, freighted silence.)

LARRY: Connor, uh, Connor took his own life.

EVAN *(Stunned)*: He . . . what?

LARRY: This is all we found with him. He had it folded up in his pocket.

(Beat.)

You can see that he's . . . he wanted to explain it, why he was . . .

(Larry recites it from memory:)

"I wish that everything was different. I wish that I were part of something. I wish that what I said mattered to / anyone."

CYNTHIA: / Please stop it, Larry.

(Evan feels the familiar rush of panic, his hands starting to sweat.)

EVAN: But, that's, this isn't . . . I'm sorry. Connor, um, Connor didn't write this.

CYNTHIA: What does that mean?

EVAN: Connor didn't, he didn't write this.

CYNTHIA *(To Larry)*: What does he mean?

LARRY: He's obviously in shock.

EVAN: No, I just, he didn't . . .

CYNTHIA *(Pointing to the letter)*: It's right here.

EVAN: I'm sorry, but I should probably just, can I please go now?

CYNTHIA: If this isn't, if Connor didn't write this, / then . . .

LARRY: / Cynthia. Please. Calm down.

EVAN: I should go now.

CYNTHIA *(Desperate to keep him here)*: But did he say anything to
     you? / Did you see anything—?

EVAN: / I really should go.

LARRY: Cynthia, honey. This is not the time.

CYNTHIA: This is all we have. This is the only thing we have left.

LARRY: Honey. Listen to me. Please.

> *(Larry puts a hand on hers.*
> *She pulls away.*
> *She begins to break down, inconsolable.)*

Cynthia.

> *(Evan holds out the letter to them, urgently, as though he cannot*
> *get it out of his hands quickly enough.)*

EVAN: You should just, you should take it. Please.

> *(Suddenly, Cynthia gasps.)*

CYNTHIA: Larry. Look.

> *(She points to Evan's arm.)*

His cast.

(Evan looks down.
He lifts up his cast and realizes what Cynthia has seen: "Con-
nor" in a Sharpie scrawl.
Cynthia turns to Larry, her eyes welling with tears of astonishment.)

His best and most dearest friend.

FIVE

Evan and Jared, online.

JARED: Holy. Shit.

EVAN: I didn't say anything. I just, I couldn't say anything.

JARED: Holy. Fucking. Shit.

EVAN: They invited me for dinner. They want to know more stuff about Connor and me, about our "friendship."

(Elsewhere, Alana appears in a pin spot of light, online, alone.)

ALANA *(Stunned)*: Still can't believe the terrible news about @ConnorMurphy.

JARED: What are you going to tell them?

EVAN: I mean, the truth.

ALANA: I wouldn't say that we were "friends" exactly. More like acquaintances.

JARED: The truth. Really. You're going to go to the Murphys' house and explain that the only thing left they have of their son is some weird sex letter that you wrote to yourself?

ALANA: We were in Chemistry together. I'm pretty sure.

JARED: You know, you could go to jail for this. If you get caught?

EVAN: But I didn't do anything.

ALANA: He was also, he was in my English class in tenth grade. I'm almost positive.

JARED: Yeah, I hate to tell you this, Evan, but you may have already perjured yourself.

EVAN: Isn't that only when you're under oath? Like, in a court room?

JARED: Well, weren't you under oath? In a way?

EVAN: No.

ALANA: Yeah, he was definitely in my English class.

JARED: Look, do you want to listen to me or do you want to have another meltdown like last year in English when you were supposed to give that speech about Daisy Buchanan, but instead you just stood there staring at your notecards and saying, "um, um, um," over and over again like you were having a brain aneurysm?

EVAN: What do you expect me to do? Just keep lying?

JARED: I didn't say, "lie." All you have to do is just nod and confirm. Whatever they say about Connor, you just nod your head and you say, yeah, that's true. Don't contradict and don't make shit up. It's foolproof. Literally, *nothing* I tell my parents is true and they have no idea.

ALANA: Three days ago, Connor Murphy was here and now . . . now he's gone.

EVAN: They were so sad. His parents? His mom was just . . . I've never seen anyone so sad before.

JARED: Well, then good thing you're about to tell her the truth about your sex letter. I'm sure that will cheer her right up.

(Evan considers this, as Alana stares out, plaintively, yearning.)

ALANA: If Connor meant something to you, please re-tweet. Or private message me if you just want to talk. At times like these, we could all use a friend.

SIX

Dinner at the Murphys.

> *Prominently, in the center of the table, a bowl of fresh apples.*
> *Evan is afraid to move or make a sound.*
> *Larry serves himself seconds.*

LARRY: Would anyone else like some more chicken?

CYNTHIA: I think you're the only one with an appetite, Larry.

LARRY *(Defensive)*: The Harrises brought it over.

CYNTHIA *(To Evan)*: Did Connor tell you about the Harrises?

(Evan nods.)

We used to go skiing together, our families.

EVAN *(Nods)*: Connor loved skiing.

ZOE: Connor hated skiing.

EVAN: Well, right. That's what I meant. Connor loved . . . talking about how much he hated skiing.

(Zoe just stares at him.)

CYNTHIA: So you guys, you . . . you hung out a lot?

EVAN: Pretty much.

ZOE: Where?

EVAN: Oh you mean, like, where did we . . . ? Well, we mostly hung out at my house. I mean, sometimes we'd come to his house if nobody else was here. We would email a lot, though, mostly. So we wouldn't have to, he didn't want to always hang out. In person, you know?

ZOE: We looked through his emails. There aren't any from you.

EVAN: Well, no, of course, yeah, I mean, that's because he had a different account. A secret account. I should have said that before. That was probably very confusing.

ZOE: Why was it secret?

EVAN: Just so that no one else could, it was more private, I guess, that way.

CYNTHIA *(To Larry)*: He knew you read his emails.

LARRY: Somebody had to be the bad guy.

(A tense pause.)

ZOE *(To Evan)*: The weird thing is, the only time I ever saw you and my brother together was when he shoved you at school last week.

CYNTHIA: He shoved you?

EVAN: I um . . . I tripped.

ZOE: I was there. I saw the whole thing. He pushed you, hard.

EVAN: *Oh.* I remember now. That was a misunderstanding. Because, the thing was, he didn't want us to talk at school, and I tried to talk to him at school. It wasn't that big a thing. It was my fault.

ZOE: Why didn't he want you to talk to him at school?

EVAN: He didn't really want people to know we were friends. I guess he was embarrassed. A little.

CYNTHIA: Why would he be embarrassed?

EVAN: Um. I guess because he thought I was sort of, you know . . .

ZOE: A nerd?

LARRY: Zoe.

ZOE: Isn't that what you meant?

EVAN: Loser, I was going to say, actually. But. Nerd works, too.

CYNTHIA: That wasn't very nice.

ZOE: Well, Connor wasn't very nice, so that makes sense.

(Cynthia takes a breath, struggles to maintain her poise.)

CYNTHIA: Connor was . . . he was a complicated person.

ZOE: No, Connor was a bad person. There's a difference.

LARRY: Zoe, please.

ZOE *(To Larry)*: Don't pretend like you don't agree with me.

(Cynthia's distress grows more and more difficult for Evan to watch.)

CYNTHIA: You refuse to remember any of the good things. / You refuse to see anything positive.

ZOE: / Because there were no good things. What were the good things?

CYNTHIA: I don't want to have this conversation in front of our guest.

ZOE: What were the good things, Mom? / Tell me.

CYNTHIA: / There were good things.

(Before even thinking, Evan finds the words tumbling out.)

EVAN: I remember a lot of good things about Connor.

(All eyes turn to him at once, as he realizes what he's done.)

ZOE: Like what?
EVAN: Never mind. I shouldn't have, I'm sorry, never mind.
CYNTHIA: No, Evan. You were saying something.
EVAN: It doesn't matter. Really.
CYNTHIA: We want to hear what you have to say. Please.

(Beat.)

EVAN: Well, I was just . . . Connor and I . . . we had a really great time together, this one day, recently.

(Evan keeps talking, unsure if he's connecting or not.)

That's something good that I remember about Connor. That's what I keep thinking about. That day.

(His eyes land on the bowl of apples in front of him.)

At the apples, um . . . the apples . . . place.

(Beat.)

Anyway. It's, I knew it was stupid. I don't know why I even brought it / up.
CYNTHIA: / He took you to the orchard?

(Evan looks at Cynthia, sees the hope in her eyes. Even Zoe has turned silent.)

EVAN: Yes. He did.

CYNTHIA: When?

EVAN: Once. It was just that once. But. He said the apples there were the best.

LARRY: I thought that place closed. Years ago.

EVAN: Exactly. Which is why we were so bummed when we got there, because it was completely, it's totally closed down now.

CYNTHIA: We used to go to the orchard all the time. We'd do picnics out there. Remember that, Zoe?

ZOE: Yeah. I do.

CYNTHIA *(To Larry)*: You and Connor had that little toy plane you would fly. Until you flew it into the creek.

LARRY *(Can't help but smile)*: That was an emergency landing.

CYNTHIA *(To Evan)*: I can't believe he took you there. I bet that was fun. I bet you two, I bet you had fun.

EVAN: We did. The whole day was just . . .

FOR FOREVER

EVAN:

>*End of May or early June*
>*This picture-perfect afternoon we share*

CYNTHIA *(To Larry)*: What was the name of that ice cream place out there we loved?

LARRY: À La Mode.

CYNTHIA: That was it. À La Mode. And they had that home-made hot fudge . . .

EVAN:

>*Drive the winding country road*
>*Grab a scoop at "À La Mode" and then . . . we're there*

CYNTHIA: We'd sit in that meadow with all the sycamores. *(To Zoe)* And you and your brother would look for four leaf clovers.

EVAN:

> *An open field that's framed with trees*
> *We pick a spot and shoot the breeze like buddies do*
> *Quoting songs by our fav'rite bands*
> *Telling jokes no one understands except us two*
> *And we talk and take in the view*
>
> *All we see is sky for forever*
> *We let the world pass by for forever*
> *Feels like we could go on for forever*
> *This way*
> *Two friends on a perfect day*

LARRY: I'd completely forgotten about that place.

CYNTHIA: Well, I guess Connor didn't. *(Looks to Evan)* Did he?

EVAN:

> *We walk a while and talk about*
> *The things we'll do when we get out of school*
> *Bike the Appalachian Trail*
> *Or write a book, or learn to sail*
> *Wouldn't that be cool?*
> *There's nothing that we can't discuss*
> *Like, girls we wish would notice us but never do*
> *He looks around and says to me,*
> *"There's nowhere else I'd rather be," and I say, "Me too"*
> *And we talk and take in the view*
> *We just talk and take in the view*
>
> *All we see is sky for forever*
> *We let the world pass by for forever*

Feels like we could go on for forever
This way
This way
All we see is light for forever
'Cause the sun shines bright for forever
We could be all right for forever this way
Two friends on a perfect day

And there he goes
Racin' toward the tallest tree
From far across a yellow field
I hear him callin', "Follow me"
There we go
Wonderin' how the world might look from up so high
One foot after the other
One branch, then to another
I climb higher and higher
I climb 'til the entire sun shines on my face
And I suddenly feel the branch give way
I'm on the ground
My arm goes numb
I look around
And I see him come to get me
He's come to get me
And ev'rything's okay

All we see is sky for forever
We let the world pass by for forever
Buddy, you and I for forever this way
This way
All we see is light
'Cause the sun burns bright
We could be all right for forever this way
Two friends

EVAN *(con't)*:
>   *True friends*
>   *On a perfect day*

>   *(Cynthia slowly crosses to Evan.*
>   *She hugs him, hard.)*

CYNTHIA: Thank you, Evan. Thank you. Thank you. Thank you. Thank you.

SEVEN

Evan and Jared, online.

JARED: His parents think you were lovers. You realize that, right?

EVAN: What? Why would they think that?

JARED: Um. You were best friends but he wouldn't let you talk to him at school? And when you did, he kicked your ass? That's like the exact formula for secret gay high school lovers.

EVAN: Oh my God.

JARED: This is why I told you—what did I tell you? You just nod and confirm.

EVAN: I tried to. I just, you don't understand. I got nervous and I started talking, and then once I started, I just . . .

JARED: You couldn't stop.

EVAN *(Realizing the truth of this as he says it)*: They didn't want me to stop.

JARED: So what else did you completely fuck up?

EVAN: Nothing. Seriously.

(Beat.)

I mean, I told them we wrote emails.

JARED: Emails.

EVAN: Yeah. I told them that Connor and I, Connor had a secret email account . . .

JARED: Oh, right. One of those "secret" email accounts. Sure. For sending pictures of your penises to each other.

EVAN *(Ignoring this)*: Yeah and so I said, he had this secret account, and we would send emails to each other.

JARED: I mean, honestly? Could you be any worse at this?

EVAN *(It suddenly occurs to him)*: They're going to want to see our emails.

JARED *(Sarcastic)*: You think?

EVAN: What am I going to do?

JARED: I can do emails.

EVAN: How?

JARED: It's easy. You make up an account, backdate the emails. There's a reason I was the only CIT with key card access to the computer cluster this summer: I have skills, son.

EVAN: You would do that?

JARED: For two grand.

EVAN: Two thousand dollars?

JARED: Five hundred.

EVAN: I can give you twenty.

JARED: Fine. But you're a dick.

(Lights out on Jared.
Heidi enters Evan's bedroom, carrying a sheaf of papers, still in her work clothes.)

HEIDI: Hey you. I have some very exciting news. Look what I found online today: college scholarship essay contests. Have you heard of these?

EVAN: I think so . . .

HEIDI: NPR did a whole thing about it this morning. There are a million different ones you can do. A million different topics. I spent my whole lunch break looking these up.

(She hands him the pages, summarizing each one as she does.)

The John F. Kennedy Profile in Courage Scholarship—three thousand dollars, college of your choice. Henry David Thoreau Society, five thousand dollars . . .

EVAN: Wow.

HEIDI: College is going to be so great for you, honey. How many times in life do you get the chance to just . . . start all over again?

EVAN: No, I know.

HEIDI: You've got so much, so many wonderful things ahead of you. High school isn't always . . . the only people that like high school are cheerleaders and football players and those people all end up miserable anyway. Yeah, you're going to find yourself in college. I really think so. I mean, I wish I could go with you . . . but . . .

(Sensing Evan's lack of enthusiasm, Heidi begins to feel a bit embarrassed.)

I just thought these were . . . it seemed like a neat idea.

EVAN: It is. For sure.

HEIDI: You've always been a wonderful writer. And we're going to need all the help we can get for college. Unless your stepmother has a trust fund for you I don't know about, with all those fabulous tips she made cocktail waitressing . . .

(Evan pretends to laugh along, as Heidi struggles to find a transition.)

Hey. I, um, I got an email from your school today. About a boy who killed himself? Connor Murphy? I didn't, I had no idea.

EVAN: Oh. Yeah. Well . . . I didn't really know him.

HEIDI: You know that . . . if you ever, if you want to talk about anything . . . I realize that lately it must feel like, I'm always working or I'm in class . . .

EVAN: It's fine.

HEIDI: Well, I'm here. And if I'm not *here* here, I'm a phone call away. Or text. Email. Whatever.

EVAN: Thanks.

(Heidi, unable to ignore the obvious any longer, points to Evan's cast.)

HEIDI: All right. It says, "Connor."

EVAN: Oh. Yeah. No.

HEIDI: You said you didn't know him.

EVAN: No. I didn't. This is . . . it's a different Connor.

(Heidi sighs, relieved, as she smiles at her own anxiety.)

HEIDI: I was so worried.

EVAN: No. I'm sure.

HEIDI *(Brightening)*: Hey, you know what? How about I bag my shift next Tuesday? When's the last time we did a taco Tuesday?

EVAN: Oh. You don't have to.

HEIDI: No, you've been back at school for a week already and I've barely seen you. Maybe we could even start brainstorming those essay questions together . . .

EVAN: That would be great.

HEIDI: Oh. That's exciting. I'm excited now. Something to look forward to.

EVAN: Me too.

(Heidi picks up the bottle of pills by his bed, asks gingerly:)

HEIDI: Are you okay on refills?

EVAN: Yes.

HEIDI: Well. Don't stay up too late.

EVAN: I won't.

HEIDI: I love you.

EVAN: I love you, too.

(She stands there in the doorway for a moment, hesitating, unsettled somehow.
Finally, she shuts the door.)

EIGHT

A spotlight. Connor, wearing the clothes we last saw him in, steps into it.

SINCERELY, ME

CONNOR:

> *Dear Evan Hansen:*
> *We've been way too out of touch*
> *Things have been crazy*
> *And it sucks that we don't talk that much*
> *But I should tell you that I think of you each night*
> *I rub my nipples and start moaning with delight*

(Lights snap up on Jared, seated, typing on a laptop, as Evan stands, reading over his shoulder with dismay.)

EVAN: Why would you write that?

JARED: I'm just trying to tell the truth.

EVAN: You know, if you're not going to take this seriously—

JARED: Okay, you need to calm yourself.

EVAN: This needs to be perfect. These emails have to prove that we were actually friends. They have to be completely realistic.

JARED: There is nothing unrealistic about the love that one man feels for another.

EVAN: Just, let's go back.

JARED: In fact, some would say there's something quite beautiful . . .

EVAN: Let's go back, Jared.

CONNOR:

I gotta tell you, life without you has been hard

JARED *(Laughing)*: Hard?

CONNOR:

Has been bad

JARED *(Meh)*: Bad?

CONNOR:

Has been rough

JARED *(Just right)*: Kinky.

CONNOR:

And I miss talking about life and other stuff

JARED: Very specific.

EVAN: Shut up.

CONNOR:

> *I like my parents—*

JARED: Who says that?

CONNOR:

> *I love my parents*
> *But each day's another fight*
> *If I stop smoking drugs*
> *Then ev'rything might be all right*

JARED: "Smoking drugs"?

EVAN: Just fix it.

JARED: This isn't realistic at all. It doesn't even sound like Connor.

EVAN: I want to show that I was, like, a good friend. That I was trying to help him. You know?

JARED: Oh my God . . .

CONNOR:

> *If I stop smoking crack—*

EVAN (*Aghast*): Crack?

CONNOR:

> *If I stop smoking pot*
> *Then ev'rything might be all right*
> *I'll take your advice*
> *I'll try to be more nice*
> *I'll turn it around*
> *Wait and see*
>
> *'Cause all that it takes is a little reinvention*
> *It's easy to change if you give it your attention*
> *All you gotta do*

Is just believe you can be who you wanna be
Sincerely, me

JARED: Are we done yet?

EVAN: I can't just show them *one* email.

JARED: Okay. Please stop hyperventilating.

EVAN: I'm not hyperventilating.

JARED: You're having considerable trouble breathing.

EVAN: I'm having no trouble breathing.

JARED: Do you need a paper bag to breathe in?

EVAN: I am NOT HYPERVENTILATING.

Dear Connor Murphy:
Yes, I also miss our talks
Stop doing drugs
Just try to take deep breaths and go on walks

JARED: No . . .

EVAN:

I'm sending pictures of the most amazing trees

JARED: No . . .

EVAN:

You'll be obsessed with all my forest expertise

JARED: Absolutely not.

EVAN:

Dude, I'm proud of you
Just keep pushing through
You're turnin' around
I can see

CONNOR:

>*Just wait and see*

EVAN/CONNOR:

>*'Cause all that it takes is a little reinvention*
>*It's easy to change if you give it your attention*
>*All you gotta do*
>*Is just believe you can be who you wanna be*
>*Sincerely . . .*

EVAN:

>*Me.*

CONNOR:

>*My sister's hot.*

EVAN *(To Jared)*: What the hell?
JARED: My bad.

CONNOR:

>*Dear Evan Hansen:*
>*Thanks for ev'ry note you send*

EVAN:

>*Dear Connor Murphy:*
>*I'm just glad to be your friend*

EVAN/CONNOR:

>*Our friendship goes beyond*
>*Your av'rage kind of bond*

EVAN:

>*But not because we're gay*

CONNOR:

>*No, not because we're gay*

EVAN/CONNOR:

> *We're close but not that way*
> *The only man*
> *That I love*
> *Is my dad*

CONNOR:

> *Well, anyway*

EVAN:

> *You're getting better ev'ry day*

CONNOR:

> *I'm getting better ev'ry day*

EVAN:

> *Keep*

CONNOR:

> *Getting*

EVAN:

> *Better*

CONNOR:

> *Ev—*

EVAN:

> *—'ry*

EVAN/CONNOR/JARED:

> *Day*
> *Hey! Hey! Hey! Hey!*

EVAN/CONNOR/JARED *(con't)*:
> *'Cause all that it takes is a little reinvention*
> *It's easy to change if you give it*

EVAN/JARED:
> *Your*

CONNOR:
> *Your*

EVAN/JARED:
> *A-*

CONNOR:
> *A-*

EVAN/CONNOR/JARED:
> *-ttention*
> *All you gotta do*
> *Is just believe you can be who you wanna be*
> *Sincerely,*

CONNOR/EVAN:
> *Miss you dearly*

JARED/EVAN/CONNOR:
> *Sincerely, me*

EVAN:
> *Sincerely, me*

EVAN/CONNOR/JARED:
> *Sincerely, me*
> *Sincerely, me*

NINE

Larry and Cynthia sit in the living room, reading from a stack of printed pages.

Evan stands, anxiously awaiting some kind of response.

EVAN: These were just some of the emails I found.

(Silence.)

I mean, I can print out more. I have a lot more. Connor and I emailed all the time.

CYNTHIA: It's . . . difficult. To read these. It doesn't sound like Connor.

(Evan realizes that he's made a terrible mistake.)

EVAN: I'm sorry. I um . . . Maybe, I shouldn't have . . .

CYNTHIA: No, no. I just . . . gosh, I don't remember the last time I heard him laugh. But you two, you would . . . ?

EVAN: No, yeah, we would, we laughed all the time.

CYNTHIA: There are more of these? More emails?

EVAN: More . . . ? Yeah. There are a lot more.

CYNTHIA: We would love to see them. We would love to see everything.

(She looks to Larry, who has said nothing.)

Wouldn't we?

LARRY: Mmhmm.

(Zoe enters, freezing when she sees Evan.)

ZOE: Why are you here?

CYNTHIA: Oh Zoe. Wait until you see what Evan brought us— emails from your brother.

LARRY: How was your first day back?

ZOE *(Dry)*: Terrific. All of a sudden, everyone wants to be my friend. I'm the dead kid's sister, didn't you know?

CYNTHIA: I'm sure they mean well.

EVAN *(Taking the hint)*: I should probably go.

CYNTHIA: You're not staying for dinner?

EVAN: Oh. Well. Just. I hadn't planned on it . . .

CYNTHIA: Then we'll do another night. I can cook something for you . . .

EVAN: You don't have to.

CYNTHIA: It would be my pleasure. We would love to have you.

(Cynthia looks to Zoe and Larry for affirmation.
Neither says anything.
Larry, picking up on the tension, motions to Evan.)

LARRY: Why don't I show you out?

EVAN: Oh. Thanks.

(Evan and Larry go, as Cynthia turns to Zoe.)

CYNTHIA: So. How was band today? I bet they're happy to have you back, huh?

ZOE: You really don't have to do this, okay?

CYNTHIA: Do what?

ZOE: Just because Connor isn't here, trying to punch through my door, screaming at the top of his lungs that he's going to kill me for no reason—that doesn't mean that, all of a sudden, we're the fucking Brady Bunch.

CYNTHIA: We are all grieving in our own way. I know how much you miss your brother. We all do.

(Cynthia sets down a stack of emails on the sofa, looks at Zoe.)

You can read these when you're ready.

(Cynthia exits.
Zoe halfheartedly flips through the emails.
She puts them down, instantly dismissive.)

REQUIEM

ZOE:

> *Why should I play this game of pretend*
> *Remembering through a secondhand sorrow?*
> *Such a great son and wonderful friend*
> *Oh, don't the tears just pour?*

ZOE *(con't):*

> *I could curl up and hide in my room*
> *There in my bed still sobbing tomorrow*
> *I could give in to all of the gloom*
> *But tell me, tell me what for?*

> *Why should I have a*
> *Heavy heart?*
> *Why should I start to break in pieces?*
> *Why should I go and fall apart for you?*

> *Why*
> *Should I play the grieving girl and lie?*
> *Saying that I miss you and that my*
> *World has gone dark without your light*
> *I will sing no requiem tonight*

(Light reveals Cynthia in Connor's bedroom, sitting on his bed, reading emails.
Larry enters, stands in the doorway.)

LARRY: I'm going to bed.

CYNTHIA: Come sit with me.

LARRY *(Sighs):* Cynthia . . .

CYNTHIA: You can't stand to be in his room for five minutes.

LARRY: I'm exhausted.

CYNTHIA: You know, Larry, at some point, you're going to have to / start . . .

LARRY: / Not tonight. Please.

(She holds out one of the printed emails.)

CYNTHIA: Just read this.

(Reluctantly, Larry takes the email without even glancing at it.)

LARRY: I'll leave the light on for you.

(He goes, stepping into the hallway.)

> *I gave you the world, you threw it away*
> *Leaving these broken pieces behind you*
> *Ev'rything wasted, nothing to say*
> *So I can sing no requiem*

CYNTHIA:
> *I hear your voice and feel you near*
> *Within these words I finally find you*
> *And now that I know that you are still here*
> *I will sing no requiem tonight*

ZOE/LARRY:
> *Why should I have a heavy heart?*

ZOE:
> *Why should I say*

	CYNTHIA:
I'll keep you with me?	*I'll keep you with me*
Why should I go and	
Fall apart for you?	
	CYNTHIA/LARRY:
Why	*Ah*
Should I play the grieving	
Girl and lie?	*Ah*
Saying that I miss you	
And that	

ZOE:

   My world
   Has gone dark

   Without
   Your light
   I will sing no requiem
   Tonight

   'Cause when the villains fall
   The kingdoms never weep
   No one lights
   A candle to remember

   No, no one mourns at all
   When they lay them down
   To sleep

   So don't tell me that I
   Didn't have it right

   Don't tell me that it
   Wasn't black and white

   After all you put me through
   Don't say it wasn't true
   That you were not the monster
   That I knew

   'Cause I
   Cannot play the grieving girl and lie
   Saying that I miss you
   And that my world has gone dark . . .

LARRY:

   My world
   Has gone dark

CYNTHIA:

   I can see
   Your light

   Ah
   Ah ah

   Ah
   Ah ah

   Ah
   Ah

LARRY:

I will sing no requiem

CYNTHIA:

I will sing no requiem

ZOE:

I will sing no requiem
Tonight

CYNTHIA/LARRY:

Oh
Oh

ZOE:

Oh

ZOE/CYNTHIA/LARRY:

Oh

TEN

Evan and Alana, online.

ALANA: Evan. Hey, it's Alana. How are you? How is everything?

EVAN: Um. Fine. Thanks . . .

ALANA: Oh my God. Jared has been telling everyone about you and Connor, how close you guys were, how you were like best friends . . .

EVAN *(Troubled)*: Oh.

ALANA: Everyone is talking about how brave you've been this week.

EVAN: They are?

ALANA: I mean, anybody else in your position would be falling apart. Dana P. was crying so hard at lunch yesterday, she pulled a muscle in her face. She had to go to the hospital.

EVAN: Isn't Dana P. new this year? She didn't even know Connor.

ALANA: That's why she was crying. Because now she'll never get the chance. Connor is really bringing the school together. It's pretty incredible. People I've never talked to before, they want to talk to me now, because they know how much Connor meant to me. It's very inspiring. I actually started a blog about him, like a sort of memorial page . . .

EVAN *(Nervous for a moment)*: Were you friends with Connor, too?

ALANA: Acquaintances. But close acquaintances.

(Evan nods, relieved.)

Can I tell you something? I think part of me always knew that you guys were friends. You did a good job of hiding it. But. I don't know.

(Heidi enters.)

I could just tell.

HEIDI: Who are you talking to on the computer?

(Evan quickly shuts the laptop and Alana disappears.)

EVAN: Oh. Um. Just Jared. It was Jared.

HEIDI *(Pleased)*: It seems like you and Jared are spending more time together. I've always said he's a great friend for you . . .

EVAN: Yeah, really great.

HEIDI: I'm proud of you. Putting yourself out there.

EVAN: Thanks.

HEIDI *(Turning to go)*: Well, I'm leaving, but I left money on the table. Order anything you want, okay?

EVAN: I thought we were doing tacos tonight. Looking at the essay questions.

HEIDI *(Suddenly remembering)*: It's Tuesday. Oh my God. Oh honey. I completely forgot. Shit.

EVAN: That's okay.

(She tries quickly to put a good face on things, spinning this as a positive development.)

HEIDI: You know what? You should go ahead and take a look at the questions without me. And then if you have any ideas, you can email me, and I can write back with any ideas that I have . . . That's better anyway, isn't it? That way you can really take your time?

EVAN *(Hiding his disappointment)*: No. Yeah. For sure.

HEIDI: We can do tacos another night, Evan. We could do tomorrow night. How about tomorrow night?

EVAN: I can't tomorrow. I have . . . I'm busy.

HEIDI *(Glancing at the time)*: Shit. I'm late.

EVAN: You should go.

HEIDI: No, let's figure this out.

EVAN: It's fine.

HEIDI: Evan . . .

EVAN: I'll make dinner for myself.

(Evan exits, leaving Heidi there in his bedroom, stricken with guilt, as lights snap up on Cynthia, calling upstairs from the Murphys' kitchen.)

CYNTHIA: Dinner will be ready in ten minutes, Evan. I hope you're hungry . . .

ELEVEN

Cynthia goes as lights find Evan standing in Connor's bedroom, alone, looking around, a complete stranger.
   A long beat.
   Zoe enters.

ZOE: Why are you in my brother's room?
EVAN *(Caught by surprise)*: I was just waiting for—
ZOE: Don't your parents get upset that you're here all the time?
EVAN: Well, it's not like I'm, I'm not here all the time . . .
ZOE: Just two nights in a row.
EVAN: Well. It's just my mom and she works most nights. Or she's in class.
ZOE: Class for what?
EVAN: Legal stuff.
ZOE: Where's your dad?

EVAN: My dad is um . . . he lives in Colorado. He left when I was seven. So. He doesn't really mind either.

(Pause.
Evan stands there, awkward.)

Your parents . . . they're really great.

ZOE *(Matter of fact)*: They can't stand each other. They fight all the time.

EVAN: Everyone's parents fight.

ZOE: My dad's, like, in total denial. He didn't even cry at the funeral.

(Beat. Not knowing what to say, Evan changes the subject.)

EVAN: Your mom was saying, gluten-free lasagna for dinner. That sounds really . . .

ZOE: Inedible?

EVAN *(Laughs)*: You're lucky your mom cooks. My mom and I just order pizza most nights.

ZOE: You're lucky you're allowed to eat pizza.

EVAN: You're not allowed to eat pizza?

ZOE: We can now, I guess. My mom was Buddhist last year so we weren't allowed to eat animal products.

EVAN: She was Buddhist last year but not this year?

ZOE: That's sort of what she does. She gets into different things. For a while it was Pilates, then it was *The Secret*, then Buddhism. Now it's free-range, *Omnivore's Dilemma* . . . whatever.

EVAN: It's cool that she's interested in so much different stuff.

ZOE: She's not. That's just what happens when you're rich and you don't have a job. You get crazy.

EVAN: My mom always says, it's better to be rich than poor.

ZOE: Well your mom's probably never been rich then.

EVAN: You've probably never been poor.

(Beat.)

Oh my God. I can't believe I just said that. I'm so sorry. That was completely rude.

ZOE *(Laughs)*: Wow. I didn't realize you were actually capable of saying something that wasn't nice.

EVAN: No, I'm not. I never say things that aren't nice. I don't even *think* things like that. I'm just, I'm really sorry.

ZOE: I was impressed. You're ruining it.

EVAN: I'm sorry.

ZOE: You really don't have to keep saying that.

(Beat.)

EVAN: Okay.

(Beat.)

ZOE: You want to say it again, don't you?

EVAN: Very much so, yes.

(They smile a little.)

ZOE: You're weird.

EVAN: I know.

ZOE *(Difficult to ask)*: Why did he say that? In his note?

(Evan looks at her, unsure what she means.
She's embarrassed to have to say it out loud.)

"Because there's Zoe. And all my hope is pinned on Zoe. Who I don't even know and who doesn't know me." Why would he write that? What does that even mean?

EVAN *(Hesitates)*: Oh. Um . . .

(Zoe looks away, realizing that he doesn't have the answer. Seeing her disappointment, Evan feels compelled to offer something.)

Well, I guess—I'm not sure if this is definitely it, but he was always . . . he always thought that, maybe if you guys were closer—

ZOE: We weren't close. At all.

EVAN: No, exactly. And so he used to always say that he wished that he was. He wanted to be.

ZOE: So you and Connor, you guys would talk about me?

EVAN: Sometimes. I mean, if he brought it up. I never brought it up. Obviously. Why would I have brought it up?
   He thought you were . . . awesome.

ZOE *(Skeptical)*: He thought I was "awesome." My brother.

EVAN: Definitely.

ZOE: How?

EVAN *(Struggling to articulate this)*: Well. Like . . . whenever you have a solo. In jazz band. You close your eyes and you get this—you probably don't even know you're doing this. But you get this half smile. Like you just heard the funniest thing in the world, but it's a secret and you can't tell anybody. But then, the way you smile, it's sort of like you're letting us in on the secret, too.

*(Evan realizes he isn't getting through.
He decides to start over.)*

IF I COULD TELL HER

EVAN:

He said
There's nothing like your smile
Sort of subtle and perfect and real
He said
You never knew how wonderful
That smile could make someone feel

And he knew
Whenever you get bored
You scribble stars on the cuffs of your jeans
And he noticed
That you still fill out the quizzes
That they put in those teen magazines

But he kept it all inside his head
What he saw he left unsaid
And though he wanted to
He couldn't talk to you
He couldn't find a way
But he would always say:

"If I could tell her
Tell her ev'rything I see
If I could tell her
How she's ev'rything to me
But we're a million worlds apart
And I don't know
How I would even start
If I could tell her
If I could tell her"

ZOE: You know the first time he ever said anything nice about me? In his note. A note he wrote to you. He couldn't even say it to me.

EVAN: He wanted to. He just . . . he couldn't.

(Zoe hesitates, feels silly even asking.)

ZOE: Did he say anything else?

EVAN: About you?

ZOE: Never mind. I don't even really care / anyway . . .

EVAN: / No no, he just, he said so many things about you. I'm trying to remember the best ones.

> *He thought*
> *You looked really pretty*

(He catches himself.)

Or . . .

> *It looked pretty cool*
> *When you put indigo streaks in your hair*

ZOE *(Laughing)*: He did?

EVAN:
> *And he wondered*
> *How you learned to dance*
> *Like all the rest of the world isn't there*
>
> *But he kept it all inside his head*
> *What he saw he left unsaid*

"If I could tell her
Tell her ev'rything I see
If I could tell her
How she's ev'rything to me   ZOE:
But we're a million   *But we're a million*
Worlds apart   *worlds apart*
And I don't know how
I would even start
If I could tell her
If I could tell her . . ."

But whaddaya do
When there's this great divide?

                                                              He just seemed so
                                                              Far away . . .

And whaddaya do
When the distance is too wide?

                                                              It's like I don't know
                                                              Anything

And how do you say,
"I love you"?
I love you
I love you
I love you

But we're a million worlds apart
And I don't know how
I would even start
If I could tell her
If I could . . .

    (Evan kisses her.
    It's impulsive and rash and he does it before he even thinks about it.
    She pulls away, stunned.)

ZOE: What are you doing?

EVAN *(Fumbling for something, anything to say)*: Um . . . I just um . . .

CYNTHIA *(From off)*: Dinner's ready, guys. Guys?

ZOE: Tell them to eat without me.

(She hurries out the door.)

TWELVE

Evan and Jared, online.
  Jared laughs, utterly incredulous.
  He wears a button with Connor's face on it.

JARED: You *what?*

EVAN: I didn't mean to, it just happened.

JARED: I can't believe you tried to kiss Zoe Murphy on her brother's *bed*. After he *died*.

EVAN: Oh my God.

  (Jared points to his button.)

JARED: Hey asshole, aren't you going to say anything?

EVAN *(Noticing the button for the first time)*: Is that a button with Connor's face on it?

JARED: I'm selling them for a nominal fee at lunch tomorrow.

EVAN: You're making money off of this?

JARED: I'm not the only one. Haven't you seen the wristbands with Connor's initials on them that Sabrina Patel started selling during free period? Or the T-shirts Matt Holtzer's mom made?

EVAN *(Not interested)*: What am I going to do about Zoe?

JARED: Are you kidding? After last night? You can never walk into that house again. Besides, this whole Connor thing? In another few days, it'll be played out anyway.

EVAN: But you just said about the T-shirts and the wristbands . . .

JARED: Exactly. We are at the peak. Which is why I've got to move these buttons before the bottom drops out of the Connor Murphy memorabilia market. Because pretty soon, there will be some Third World tsunami to raise money for, and Connor will just be that dead kid whose name no one remembers.

EVAN: That's . . . that's terrible.

JARED: Hey. At least it was fun while it lasted. You got to have some quality time with your fake family, snuggle with Zoe Murphy . . .

EVAN: But that's . . . that's not why I was doing it. I was trying to help them. I just wanted to help them.

JARED: Regardless, bro. It's over. A week from now? Everybody will have already forgotten about Connor. You'll see.

(Lights on Jared snap out, as they snap up on Alana.)

ALANA: Everybody has forgotten about Connor. A week ago, the whole school was wearing those wristbands and the buttons with his face on them. People were talking to each other that never talked to each other before. And now . . . it's all gone. Completely. You were his best friend. You can't let this happen.

EVAN: Well, I know, but . . .

ALANA *(Lightbulb)*: Maybe you can ask Zoe to do something. Or maybe you guys could do something together.

EVAN: Zoe?

ALANA: Yeah, she's the perfect person to help get people interested again. You guys could write something together for the blog . . .

EVAN: Yeah, it's just . . . I don't know if that's the best way for us to get people to remember him . . .

ALANA: Well, I can guarantee you that if you don't do something, then *no one* will remember him. Is that what you want?

EVAN *(Struggling to respond)*: But I'm just . . .

(Alana, exasperated by his indecisiveness, exits in a huff. Evan sits there, alone.)

What am I supposed to do?

CONNOR: Why don't you talk to Zoe?

*(And suddenly Connor is there beside him.
There is nothing spectral or spooky about Connor's presence, and Evan is not at all surprised to see him.)*

EVAN: I can't talk to Zoe. I already ruined everything with Zoe.

CONNOR *(Dismissive)*: Says who? Jared? Why are you even talking to Jared about this?

EVAN: Who else am I supposed to talk to?

CONNOR: You can talk to me.

(Evan laughs, a ridiculous idea.)

Unless you have other options.

(Evan realizes he has none.)

EVAN: I don't know what to do.

CONNOR: Look. Zoe, my parents . . . they need you. You're the only person who can make sure everybody doesn't just forget me.

(Beat.)

Oh right. They already did.

EVAN *(Empathetic)*: After two whole weeks.

CONNOR: And once they've forgotten about me, what do you think happens to you? I mean, nobody cares about people like us.

EVAN: "People like us"?

CONNOR: Connor Murphy: the kid who threw a printer at Mrs. G. in second grade. Or Evan Hansen: the kid who stood outside a jazz band concert trying to talk to Zoe Murphy, but his hands were too sweaty. You know. People like that. Look:

DISAPPEAR

CONNOR:

Guys like you and me
We're just the losers who keep waiting to be seen

Right? I mean . . .

No one seems to care
Or stops to notice that we're there
So we get lost in the in-between

But, if you can somehow keep them thinking of me
And make me more than an abandoned memory

Well, that means we matter too
It means someone will see that you are there

No one deserves to be forgotten
No one deserves to fade away
No one should come and go
And have no one know
He was ever even here
No one deserves
To disappear, to disappear
Disappear

EVAN *(Beginning to be convinced)*: It's true.

CONNOR:

    Even if you've always been that
    Barely-in-the-background kind of guy

EVAN/CONNOR:

    You still matter

CONNOR:

    And even if you're somebody who can't escape the
    Feeling that the world's passed you by

EVAN:

    You still matter

CONNOR:

    If you never get around to doing some remarkable thing

EVAN/CONNOR:

    That doesn't mean . . .

EVAN:

That you're not worth remembering

CONNOR:

Think of the people who
Need to know

EVAN:

They need to know

So you need
To show them

I need to
show them

CONNOR/EVAN:

That no one deserves to be forgotten

EVAN:

No one deserves to be forgotten

CONNOR/EVAN:

No one deserves to fade away

EVAN:

To fade away

CONNOR/EVAN:

No one should flicker out
Or have any doubt
That it matters that they are here

EVAN:

No one deserves

CONNOR:

No one deserves

EVAN/CONNOR:

> *To disappear*
> *To disappear, disappear*

CONNOR:

> *When you're fallin' in a forest*
> *And there's nobody around*
> *All you want is for somebody to find you*
> *You're fallin' in a forest*
> *And when you hit the ground*
> *All you need is for somebody to find you*

(And Connor is gone.
Evan, now at school, speaks to Alana and Jared, sharing a home-made pamphlet with them.)

EVAN: I'm calling it The Connor Project.

JARED *(Skeptical)*: The Connor Project.

EVAN: A student group dedicated to keeping Connor's memory alive, to showing that everybody should matter, everybody is important.

ALANA: I am so honored. I would love to be vice president of The Connor Project.

EVAN: Vice president?

ALANA: You're right. We should be co-presidents.

EVAN *(Just pleased she said yes)*: Yeah. No. Definitely. That works for me.

ALANA *(To Jared)*: You can be treasurer or secretary. Unfortunately, the co-president position has already been filled.

JARED: Well, shit. I guess I'm going to have to order new buttons. Unless you think I can squeeze the words "Connor Project" onto the old buttons . . . I mean, depending on the font size . . .

EVAN *(To Jared)*: Do you actually think we should do this?

(Alana answers for him.)

ALANA: Are you kidding, Evan? We have to do this. Not just for Connor. For . . . everyone.

(Evan, emboldened by the success, allows a small smile.)

EVAN:
>'Cause no one deserves to be forgotten

ALANA/JARED:
>No one deserves to fade away

EVAN:
>No one deserves to fade away

(Jared hands each of them a button, unable to resist getting caught up in the excitement.
Lights shift and Evan, Alana, and Jared are with the Murphys at their kitchen table, Cynthia and Larry eagerly perusing a pamphlet.)

We're calling it The Connor Project.
CYNTHIA *(Trying it out)*: The Connor Project.
EVAN: Imagine a major online presence.
ALANA: With links to educational materials.
JARED: A massive fundraising drive . . .
EVAN: . . . to help people like Connor.
ALANA: And for the kickoff event, an all-school memorial assembly next week. Students, teachers, whoever wants to, they can get up and talk about Connor, talk about his legacy.

(Cynthia and Larry share a look.)

CYNTHIA: I don't know what to say.

LARRY: I didn't realize Connor meant this much to people.

ALANA: Oh my God. He was one of my closest acquaintances. He was my lab partner in Chemistry, and we presented together on *Huck Finn* in tenth grade. He was so funny. He kept calling it . . . well instead of "*Huck*" *Finn* . . .

(From Larry and Cynthia's faces, she thinks better of finishing the story.)

Nobody else in our class thought of that.

(Evan turns to Zoe, cautiously, testing the waters.)

EVAN: For the assembly, I was thinking maybe the jazz band could do something . . .

ZOE: Oh. Yeah. Maybe.

JARED: Great idea, Evan.

(Evan glares at him.)

EVAN: Thank you, Jared.

JARED: No sweat.

CYNTHIA: Oh, Evan . . . this is just, this is wonderful.

(Cynthia takes Evan's hand, unable to express her gratitude adequately in words.)

No one deserves to be forgotten

EVAN:

No one deserves to fade away

CYNTHIA/JARED/ALANA:
>*No one deserves to disappear*

(Lights shift, as Larry, Cynthia, and Zoe exit.)

EVAN:
>*No one deserves to disappear*

ALANA/JARED/EVAN:
>*No one should*
>*Flicker out or have any doubt*
>*That it matters that they are here*

EVAN:
>*No one deserves*

      ALANA:
      >*No one deserves*

          JARED:
          >*No one deserves*

EVAN/JARED/ALANA:
>*To disappear*
>*To disappear*

EVAN/JARED:
>*Disappear*

ALANA:
>*No one deserves*
>*To be forgotten* JARED:
        >*To disappear* EVAN:
              >*Disappear*
>*Disappear*   *Disappear*   *Disappear*

(Jared and Alana exit as lights shift to find Evan standing in Connor's bedroom.
Cynthia holds out a nondescript necktie.)

CYNTHIA: For tomorrow. For the assembly.

EVAN *(Unsure of what she means)*: Oh.

CYNTHIA: When Connor started seventh grade, all my girl-friends said, here comes Bar Mitzvah season. He's going to have a different party every Saturday. I took him to get a suit, some shirts . . . a tie.

(Beat.)

He didn't get invited to a single one.

(She extends the tie to Evan.)

I thought you could wear this for your speech.

(Evan goes cold, the familiar tingling sensation returning to his palms.)

EVAN: My what?

CYNTHIA: Well, Alana said that anyone who wanted to would have a chance to say something tomorrow. I think we all assumed that you would be the first to sign up.

EVAN: I don't, um . . . the thing is just, I don't really do very well with, um, with public speaking. I'm not very good at it. You wouldn't want me to. Trust me.

CYNTHIA: Of course I would want you to. I'm sure the whole school wants to hear from you. I know Larry and I do, and Zoe . . .

(Evan says nothing.
She puts the tie in his hands.)

Think about it.

(She exits.
Evan sits there for a moment, staring at the tie, paralyzed.
Finally, he stands.
He slowly puts on the tie, a certain reverence to this.)

ZOE/CYNTHIA/ALANA:
To disappear
Disappear

To disappear   JARED/LARRY:
                       Disappear

Disappear

                       Disappear

ALANA/JARED:
To disappear   LARRY:
                    Disappear   ZOE/CYNTHIA:
                                        Disappear

Disappear
                    Disappear
                                        Disappear

To disappear
                    Disappear
                                        Disappear

(Evan takes a deep, deep breath.
He reaches into his back pocket and pulls out a handful of note
cards.
He turns and the lights shift.
The school auditorium.

Evan stands there, utterly alone on an empty, endless stage, star-ing out into the darkness, the note cards shaking in his trembling hands.
He begins slowly, tentative, terrified.)

EVAN: Good morning, students and faculty. I would, um, I would just like to say a few words to you today about . . . my best friend . . . Connor Murphy.

I'd like to tell you about the day that we went to the old Autumn Smile Apple Orchard. Connor and I, we stood under an oak tree, and Connor said, he wondered what the world would look like from all the way up there. So we decided to find out. We started climbing slowly, one branch at a time. When I finally looked back, we were already thirty feet off the ground. Connor just looked at me and smiled, that way he always did. And then . . . well, then I . . .

(His palms begin to sweat.
He nervously wipes them on his shirt.
It doesn't help.)

. . . I fell.

(His anxiety only builds, as he continues to wipe his hands.)

I lay there on the ground and then—

(He turns to the next card.)

Good morning, students and faculty, I would um . . .

(A shiver of panic goes down his spine as he realizes that he has lost his place in the note cards.
He tries frantically to put them back in order.)

Um . . . um . . . um . . .

(Suddenly, a card drops from his hands, fluttering slowly to the ground.
He crouches to pick it up.
There on the ground, Evan suddenly stops.
He stares out past the lights at the faces in the auditorium.
A moment of pure, unadulterated terror grips him.
Everything is telling him to run away.
A long beat.
He looks at the tie.
He makes a decision.
Slowly, he stands, putting away the cards entirely.
He begins once again, differently.)

YOU WILL BE FOUND

EVAN:

> *Have you ever felt like nobody was there?*
> *Have you ever felt forgotten in the middle of nowhere?*
> *Have you ever felt like you could disappear?*
> *Like you could fall, and no one would hear*

(The story he has told so many times before becomes, now, suddenly, a genuine discovery.)

But see, the thing is, when I looked up . . . Connor was there. That's the gift that he gave me. To show me that I wasn't alone. To show me that I matter. That everybody does. That's the gift that he gave all of us. I just wish . . . I wish we could have given that to him.

> *So, let that lonely feeling wash away*
> *Maybe there's a reason to believe you'll be okay*

'Cause when you don't feel strong enough to stand
You can reach, reach out your hand

And oh, someone will come runnin'
And I know they'll take you home

Even when the dark comes crashin' through
When you need a friend to carry you
And when you're broken on the ground
You will be found
So let the sun come streamin' in
'Cause you'll reach up and you'll rise again
Lift your head and look around
You will be found
You will be found
You will be found
You will be found
You will be found

(Suddenly, onstage, the screens begin to hum and buzz to life.
Alana enters.)

ALANA: Have you seen this? Someone put a video of your speech online.

EVAN: My speech?

(Jared enters.)

ALANA: People started sharing it, I guess, and now . . . I mean, Connor is / everywhere.

JARED: / Your speech is everywhere. This morning, The Connor Project page, it only had fifty-six people following it.

(Cynthia enters.)

EVAN: How many does it have now?

JARED: Four thousand, / five hundred, eighty-two.

CYNTHIA: / Sixteen thousand, two hundred, and thirty-nine.

EVAN: I don't understand. What happened?

CYNTHIA: You did.

(The image of Evan's speech begins to proliferate, spreading across screens, one, two, many Evan Hansens.

Evan, Cynthia, Alana, and Jared stand among the images, awash in the images, engulfed by them.

The space slowly fills with people's posts, a Virtual Community.

The Voices overlap and each of the individual threads becomes part of the larger stream of messages and one by one they fuse with the stream until there is no separation between them.

A dreamlike feel, like we have fallen into some kind of collective hallucination.

Maybe this is what life after death feels like or maybe what it would feel like to fall into the internet.)

ALANA:

There's a place where we don't have to feel unknown

(Separate Voices, one at a time, emerge to speak, to commune with one another.)

VOICES:

Oh my God

Everybody needs to see this

ALANA:

And ev'ry time that you call out you're a little less alone

VOICES:

I can't stop watching this video

Seventeen years old

90

JARED:
> *If you only say the word*

VOICES:
Take five minutes, this will make your day

ALANA/JARED:
> *From across the silence your voice is heard*

VOICES:	VIRTUAL VOICES/
Share it with the people	CYN/Z/A/J/L:
you love	*Oh*

Re-post

The world needs to hear this

A beautiful tribute

Favorite

I know someone who really	
needed to hear this today, so	
thank you, Evan Hansen,	*Oh*
for doing what you're doing	

I never met you, Connor.	
But coming on here, reading	A/CYN/L/VV:
everyone's posts . . .	*Oh*

z/vv/J:

It's so easy to feel alone,	*Oh*
but Evan is exactly right,	
we're not alone	

	Someone will
None of us	*Come runnin'*

VOICES *(con't)*:
We're not alone

None of us

None of us

None of us is alone   A/CYN/L: Z/J:

Like
                                                    Oh
                                                                        Oh

Forward

Share.

Especially now, with everything you
hear in the news . . .

Like

Share

Re-post

Forward
                                                                        Oh

Thank you, Evan Hansen,   *Someone will*
for giving us a space   *Come runnin'*
to remember Connor

To be together   *Oh*

To find each other

VOICES: Share		z/j:	
Sending prayers from Michigan		*Someone will* *Come runnin'*	
Vermont			
Tampa	J:	z/L:	
Sacramento	*To take* *You home*	*To take* *You home*	
Thank you Evan Hansen			
Re-post			A/CYN: *Someone will* *Come runnin'* *To take*
Thank you, Evan			*You home*

Watch until the end

Thank you, Evan Hansen

This video is everything right now

Thank you, Evan

All the feels.

This is about community

The meaning of friendship

VOICES:	J:	Z/L:	A/CYN:
Thank you			
Thanks to Evan	*To take*		
	You home	*To take*	
Evan Hansen	*Oh*	*You home*	*Home*

Thank you, Evan Hansen

ALL:

> *Even when the dark comes crashin' through*
> *When you need a friend to carry you*
> *When you're broken on the ground*
> *You will be found*
> *So let the sun come streamin' in*
> *'Cause you'll reach up and you'll rise again*
> *If you only look around*
> *You will be found*

H/A:

> *You will be found*

CYN/Z/VV/L: J:
> *You will be found*   *You will be found*

H/A:

> *You will be found*

> *You will be found*

(*Photographs of Connor begin to appear on the screens, mingling with the images of Evan.*)

ALL (*Except for Evan and Larry*):
> *Out of the shadows*
> *The morning is breaking*

And all is new
All is new

ALL *(With Evan)*:
It's filling up the empty
And suddenly I see

That all is new
All is new

(As the darkness lifts, something inside of Larry shifts.
He stares up at the screens, images of his son surrounding him.
He turns to Cynthia.
He can no longer hold back his emotion.
In an instant, all of his defenses, all of the hurt and anger calcified
over years, decades—all of it shatters at once, irrevocably.
He breaks down.
Cynthia holds him.
They stand there, surrounded by light, holding one another.)

A/J:
You are not alone

A/J/Z/CON:
You are not alone

A/J/Z/CON/CYN/L/H/VV:
You are not alone
You are not alone

A/Z/VV/CON/L:
You are not alone

CYN/VV/J/H:
You are not alone

A/Z/VV/CON/L:
You are not alone

You are not alone

You are not

A/Z/CON/L:

CYN/H:

J:

You are

You are

You are not

Not alone

Not alone

You are

Not alone

(Zoe sits on Connor's bed, staring at a laptop screen, her expression unreadable, as the screens around her continue to swirl and pulse.)

Z:
Even when the dark comes crashin' through
When you need someone to carry you
When you're broken on the ground

VV/A/H/CYN/J/CON/L:
You will be found

E/Z:
So let the sun come streamin' in

ALL:
'Cause you'll reach up and you'll rise again

VV/A/CYN/J/CON/L/H:
If you only look around

A/CYN/CON/H: Z/E/L:
You will be found

                                           Even when the dark
                                           Comes crashin' through

A/VV/CYN/CON/H/L:
You will be found

                                           When you need someone
                                           To carry you

VV/A/H/CYN/J/L/CON:
    You will be found
    You will be found

    (The music cuts out, sharply.
    Evan sits beside Zoe on Connor's bed.)

ZOE: Everything you said in your speech. Everything you've done. You don't know how much . . . what you've given . . . all of us, everyone. My family. Me.
EVAN *(Uncomfortable)*: No, I . . . this is . . .
ZOE: You've given me my brother back.

    (Without warning, she kisses him.
    Stunned, he pulls away for a moment.
    He knows that this is the point of no return.
    There is no going back.
    He makes a decision.
    He kisses her.
    They kiss.
    They are reeling.
    The world is reeling.)

ACT TWO

ONE

Once again, we hear the murmuring of voices, as the house lights slowly fade.

> *Once again, the screens buzz with text.*
> *All of it now about Connor Murphy.*
> *His absence fills the world.*
> *The murmuring grows louder and louder when suddenly everything goes black.*
> *Lights snap up on Alana in her bedroom, speaking into her laptop screen.*

ALANA: Hey everybody, it's me Alana, Connor Project co-president, associate treasurer, media consultant, chief technology officer, and assistant creative director slash public policy director for creative public policy initiatives for The Connor Project.

(Lights find Evan in his bedroom, speaking into his laptop screen, something unmistakably different about him, a newfound confidence.)

EVAN: Hi I'm Evan. I'm co-president of The Connor Project.

(Pause.)

ALANA: Wish I could see all of your amazing faces out there.

EVAN: Hope you're having an amazing day.

ALANA: Now, I know a lot of you guys have seen the inspirational videos on our website.

EVAN: Thank you for checking out the awesome new videos we put up this week with Mr. and Mrs. Murphy, Connor's sister, / Zoe . . .

ALANA: / . . . and Connor's best friend, my co-president: Evan Hansen.

EVAN: As you know, Connor's favorite place in the entire world was the incredible Autumn Smile Apple Orchard.

ALANA: The stunning Autumn Smile Apple Orchard, which tragically closed seven years ago.

(Alana posts a current photo of the abandoned orchard, an empty overgrown field dotted with tree stumps, a large FOR SALE sign nailed to a rotting fence.)

EVAN: Connor loved trees.

ALANA: Connor was *obsessed* with trees. He and Evan used to spend hours together sitting at the orchard, looking at the trees . . . *being* with the trees, sharing fun facts they knew about the trees.

EVAN: But the one thing Connor wished more than anything was that some day the orchard would be brought back to life.

ALANA: Which is where you come in . . .

(Alana posts a digital architectural rendering of a blossoming orchard nestled in an idyllic park.)

EVAN: Because today we are starting a major / Kickstarter campaign.

ALANA: / One of the most ambitious Kickstarter initiatives since the internet was first created to raise—gulp—fifty thousand dollars . . .

EVAN: . . . fifty thousand dollars in three weeks.

ALANA: It's a lot of money, I know. But it's also a lot of amazing. So let's do it, guys, and . . .

ALANA/EVAN: . . . make The Connor Murphy Memorial Orchard not just a dream . . .

EVAN: . . . but / a rea—

ALANA *(Louder than Evan)*: / But a reality.

TWO

A spotlight.

  Connor steps into it.

SINCERELY, ME (REPRISE)

CONNOR:

  Dear Evan Hansen:
  Life at rehab is all right
  I like the yoga
  And the sharing circles ev'ry night
  But, dude, these stories sometimes scare you half to death
  So many people end up sucking dick for meth

  (Lights snap up on Jared, elsewhere, typing on his computer, enjoying himself immensely.

Evan, sitting at his laptop in his bedroom, shakes his head, chagrined.)

> *Oh, and one more thing*
> *That's worth mentioning . . .*
> *That guy from our school, Jared Kleinman?*
> *Yes, the insanely cool Jared Kleinman!*
> *I think we should start*
> *And make him a part*
> *Of this awesome friendship we have*

(Jared shuts his laptop and joins Connor.)

CONNOR/JARED:

> *A part of this awesome friendship we have*

CONNOR:

> *This adorably heartwarming friendship we have*

JARED:

> *Hey!*

CONNOR:

> *Hey!*

CONNOR/JARED:

> *Hey hey hey hey!*
> *'Cause all that it takes is a little—*

(Unable to take any more of this, Evan stands, and the music cuts out.)

EVAN: Okay. No, Jared. Obviously not.

(Jared and Connor turn to look at Evan, confused, unsure what he finds objectionable.)

JARED: What? What's the problem?

EVAN: You weren't friends with him. That's not part of the story. I was his only friend. You know that. You can't just make things up. You need to redo it.

(Jared escorts his imagined Connor offstage.)

JARED: You're totally right. I mean, what was I thinking, just making things up in a completely fabricated email exchange that never happened?

EVAN: Just don't change the story please, okay?

JARED: Well, if you want me to redo this email, you're going to have to wait until Monday, because I have plans all weekend with my camp friends. Or, as I like to call them: my real friends.

EVAN: Yeah, actually, I think we're good on the emails for now. We're kind of focusing on bigger stuff. The orchard. Things like that.

JARED: Oh. Well, I can definitely do more with the Kickstarter. I mean, I am the treasurer.

EVAN: I think Alana and I are pretty much set on that. I'll let you know if I think of anything, though.

JARED: Got it. Hey, I bet Zoe's happy that your cast is gone.

EVAN: I guess.

JARED: I mean, talk about killing the mood, right? Having to see your brother's name written on your boyfriend's arm all the time?

EVAN: I'm not her . . . I don't know what we are.

JARED: Don't even worry about it, bro. The only thing you should be worrying about right now is building that orchard for Connor. Because, if there was one thing about

Connor: the guy loved trees. Or, no, wait, *you* love trees.
That's weird. Isn't that weird?

*(Evan doesn't respond.
Heidi enters in scrubs.)*

HEIDI: What are you up to?

(Evan shuts the computer and Jared vanishes.)

EVAN: Nothing much.

HEIDI: I feel like, every time I come into your room, you shut
your computer screen.

EVAN: Not really.

HEIDI: I don't know what you do on there that you don't want
me to see.

EVAN: I was doing homework, Mom.

(Evan stands, begins packing up his things.)

HEIDI: Do you have a minute?

EVAN: Well, actually, I was about to go to Jared's.

HEIDI: Didn't you go to Jared's last night?

EVAN: Well, yeah, we're doing a Spanish project together.
We're going to be working late again, though, so I'll probably just stay over.

HEIDI: I saw the strangest thing on Facebook today.

EVAN: Oh really?

HEIDI: There was a video from the, uh, something called The,
uh, Connor Project? Have you heard of that?

(Evan freezes.)

Because their website, it says that you're the president.

EVAN *(Quietly)*: Co-president.

HEIDI: Uh-huh. Well, this was, it was a video of you doing a speech? About that boy. Connor Murphy. How you climbed a tree together.

(Evan sits there, silent, unsure what to do, his old anxiety suddenly returning, his hands beginning to tingle.)

EVAN: I just, um . . . I don't, um . . .

HEIDI: You told me you didn't know him. That boy?

EVAN: I know. But.

HEIDI: But then in your speech, you said he was your best friend.

EVAN: Well, because it wasn't true. When I . . .

(He hesitates for just a moment.
The perfect opportunity to tell the truth.
He makes his choice.)

When I said I didn't know him.

HEIDI: So you broke your arm with him? At an orchard?

(Evan nods.)

You told me you broke your arm at work. At the park.

EVAN: Who do you think drove me to the hospital? Who do you think waited with me in the emergency room for three hours? You were at work, remember? I couldn't even, you didn't answer your phone.

HEIDI: You told me your boss took you to the hospital.

EVAN: Well, so, I lied, obviously.

HEIDI: When were you planning on telling me any of this? Or you weren't?

EVAN: When would I tell you, exactly? When are you even here?

HEIDI: I'm here right now.

EVAN: One night a week? Most people, their parents, they try to do a little bit better than that, just so you know.

HEIDI: Isn't that lucky for them.

EVAN: I have to go to Jared's.

HEIDI: I don't think I want you going out right now actually.

EVAN: I told Jared I would be at his house ten minutes ago.

HEIDI: All right, listen. I am missing class tonight so I can be here to talk to you, Evan. I would like you to please just talk to me.

EVAN: Okay. I mean, I can't just not do work for school because you decided to miss class. I can't just stop everything whenever you decide it's convenient for you.

HEIDI: I don't understand what is going on with you.

EVAN: Nothing is going on with me.

HEIDI: You're standing up in front of the school and giving *speeches*? You're president of a group? I don't know who that person is.

EVAN: You're making a big deal out of something that isn't a big deal.

HEIDI *(Increasingly desperate)*: What is going on with you? / You need to talk to me. You need to communicate with me.

EVAN: / Nothing is going on with me. I told you everything.

HEIDI: I'm your mother. I'm your mother.

(The word catches in her throat.
Silence.
Evan says nothing.
Finally, Heidi composes herself.)

I'm sorry. I was . . . I don't know why I . . . I'm happy. I'm happy you had a friend, sweetheart. I'm just so sorry he's gone. I wish I had known.

(Evan nods, suddenly ashamed.)

If you ever want to talk about it . . .

EVAN: I should go.

(*Evan turns to leave.*
Heidi picks up a bottle of pills.)

HEIDI: You okay on refills?

EVAN: I'm not taking them anymore.

HEIDI (*Surprised*): Oh.

EVAN: I haven't needed them.

HEIDI: Really? So, no anxiety or . . . ? Even with everything that's . . . ?

EVAN: I've been fine.

HEIDI: Well, great. That's great. It's . . . I'm proud of you. I guess those letters to yourself must have really helped, huh?

EVAN: I guess so.

HEIDI: Well. Don't stay up too late. It's a school night.

EVAN: I won't.

(*Evan goes.*
Heidi stands there, utterly at sea.)

THREE

The Murphys' garage.
    Larry digs through an old cardboard box, taking out a number of signed baseballs in protective plastic cases.

LARRY: Brooks Robinson. Jim Palmer. Here's the entire '96 team. Look at that.

EVAN: Wow.

LARRY: You get the right people to come to an auction like this, baseball fans, I bet you could raise a thousand bucks for the orchard, easy.

EVAN: No, it's a great idea. I'm definitely going to talk to Alana about it.

    (Larry pulls out a baseball glove from the box, sets it aside, continues rummaging.

Inside the baseball glove, a can of shaving cream and some rubber bands—the beginnings of a project that was never finished.)

LARRY: I swear, I have a Cal Ripken in here somewhere . . .

EVAN: This is really generous of you. To donate all this stuff.

(Zoe enters. She and Evan share a furtive smile.)

ZOE *(To Larry)*: Mom says that your show is on and she doesn't
    want to DVR it again.

LARRY: Well, tell her we're busy.

ZOE: With what?

EVAN: Your dad had a good idea for the orchard. To do an auction.

LARRY: Evan's helping me go through my collection here.

(Beat.)

ZOE: Dad, are you torturing him?

LARRY: What?

ZOE: Evan, is he torturing you?

EVAN: No. What?

ZOE: You can tell him he's being boring and you want to leave.
    He won't be upset.

LARRY: He can leave whenever he wants.

EVAN: I don't want to leave.

ZOE: Evan, do you want to leave?

LARRY *(To Evan)*: If you want to leave . . .

EVAN: I don't want to leave.

ZOE: Okay. Well. Don't say I didn't warn you . . .

(Zoe exits.)

LARRY *(Laughs)*: Women. Right?

(Evan attempts to laugh along, one of the guys.)

EVAN: I know.

LARRY *(Gingerly)*: So, you and Zoe . . . ?

EVAN *(Desperate to avoid the subject)*: This glove is really cool. Wow.

(Evan picks it up.)

LARRY: You feel how stiff the leather is?

EVAN: For sure.

LARRY: Never been used. You probably have your own glove at home, I'm sure.

EVAN: Oh. Uh. Somewhere. I don't know if it fits anymore. It's been a while.

LARRY: You know what? Why don't you take this one?

EVAN: Oh. No. I couldn't.

LARRY: Why not? Because, it sounds like, I mean, if you need a new glove anyway . . . This one is just going to sit here, collecting dust.

EVAN: Are you sure?

TO BREAK IN A GLOVE

LARRY:

> *I bought this glove a thousand years ago*
> *For some birthday*
> *Or some Christmas that has come and gone*
> *I thought we might play catch or—I don't know*
> *But he left it in the bag with the tag still on*

You'd have to break it in, though, first. You can't catch anything with it that stiff.

EVAN: How do you break it in?

LARRY: Your dad never taught you how to break in a baseball glove?

EVAN: I guess not.

LARRY:

> *It's all a process that is really quite precise*
> *A sort of secret method known to very few*
> *So, if you're in the market for . . . professional advice*
> *Well, today could be a lucky day for you*

Shaving cream.

EVAN: Shaving cream?

LARRY: Oh yeah. You rub that in for about five minutes. Then you tie it all up with rubber bands, put it under your mattress, and sleep on it. And then the next day, you repeat. And you've got to do it for at least a week. Every day. Consistent.

> *And though this method isn't easy*
> *Ev'ry second that you spend*
> *Is gonna pay off*
> *It'll pay off in the end*
>
> *It just takes a little patience*
> *It takes a little time*
> *A little perseverance*
> *And a little uphill climb*
> *You might not think it's worth it*
> *You might begin to doubt*
> *But you can't take any shortcuts*
> *You gotta stick it out*
> *And it's the hard way*
> *But it's the right way*

The right way
To break in a glove

Nowadays, with your generation, I hate to say it, but it's all about instant gratification. Who wants to read a book when you can read the Facebook instead?
EVAN: Totally.

(Larry picks up the shaving cream and the rubber bands.)

LARRY: With something like this, you have to be ready to put in the work. Make the commitment.

(Beat.)

What do you think?
EVAN: I mean, definitely.

(Evan puts out a hand.
Larry sprays shaving cream onto it.
He sprays shaving cream onto his own hand and begins working the glove.)

LARRY:
     Some people say, "Just use a microwave
     Or try that run-it-through-hot-water technique"

(He laughs.)

     Well, they can gloat about the time they save
     'Til they gotta buy another glove next week

(Evan smiles.
They begin to work together on the glove as their voices join.)

LARRY:

It just takes a little patience   EVAN:

                                                It takes a little patience

It takes a little time

                                                It takes a little time

A little perseverance

                                                Perseverance

And
A little uphill climb   *A little uphill climb*
And it's the hard way
But it's the right *way*
The right way   *The right way*

'Cause there's a right way
In ev'rything you do
Keep that grit

                                                Keep that grit
Follow through   *Follow through*

LARRY:

    Even when ev'ryone around you thinks you're crazy
    Even when ev'ryone around you lets things go
    Whether you're prepping for some test
    Or you're miles from some goal
    Or you're just trying to do what's best
    For a kid who's lost control

(Larry stops, surprised by his sudden emotion.)

    You do the hard thing
    'Cause that's the right thing
    Yeah, that's the right thing

EVAN: Connor was really lucky. To have a dad that . . . a dad who cared so much. About . . . taking care of stuff.

(Larry collects himself.)

LARRY: Your dad must feel pretty lucky to have a son like you.

(Evan lies—a reflex.)

EVAN: Yeah. He does.
LARRY: Good.

(Beat.)

Well. If you want to go catch up with Zoe . . .

*(Evan nods, begins to exit.
He stops, unable to let the lie stand.)*

EVAN: I don't know why I said that. About my dad. It's not true.
My parents got divorced when I was seven. My dad moved
to Colorado. He and my step-mom, they have their own
kids now. So. That's sort of his priority.

*(Pause.
Larry puts the glove in Evan's hands, a hand on his shoulder.)*

LARRY: Shaving cream. Rubber bands. Mattress. Repeat. Got it?
EVAN: Got it.

LARRY:
It's the hard way

The right way
To break in a glove

EVAN:
But it's the right *way*
The right way
To break in a glove

You're good to go.

FOUR

Evan's bedroom.
   Zoe slowly walks around, taking it in.
   Evan hovers, nervously watching.
   A palpable tension between them.

ZOE: So when does your mom get off work?

EVAN: She has class Sunday nights, so she won't be home for another few hours.

ZOE: We have the whole house to ourselves?

EVAN: You know it.

ZOE: We should throw a kegger.

EVAN: We should definitely throw a kegger. For sure.

ZOE: Until your mom comes home.

EVAN: In three hours.

   (Pause.)

Thank you for, um, for coming.

ZOE: You realize, I've been asking to come to your house for, like, weeks, and every time you've immediately said no.

EVAN: I know. Which is why I appreciate that you're here now.

(Zoe glances at papers on his desk.)

ZOE: What are all these?

EVAN *(Hurries to put them away)*: Oh. Those are, my mom is obsessed with these college scholarship essay contests she found online. She keeps printing out more of them.

ZOE: There are so many.

EVAN: Yeah. I know. I mean, I'd have to win probably a hundred of them to actually pay for college. When you add it all up. Tuition, housing, books.

ZOE: Your parents, they can't . . . ?

EVAN: Not really.

ZOE: I'm sorry.

(Evan shrugs.
Uncomfortable, he changes the subject.)

EVAN: Well, hey, I meant to tell you before, we had a meeting with The Connor Project a few days ago and I think we have a really great strategy for raising more money for the orchard.

ZOE: We, um . . . can we talk?

EVAN *(Crestfallen)*: Oh. Shit.

ZOE: What?

EVAN: No. Just. You're breaking up with me, right? That's why you came over.

ZOE: Breaking up with you?

EVAN: God. Like, how presumptuous can I get? I don't even know if we're, like, dating officially or whatever, which isn't even . . . never mind, why am I even talking right now? It's fine. Don't worry, you can tell me, I'm not going to *cry* or start breaking things . . .

(Zoe just stares at him.)

ZOE: I'm not breaking up with you.
EVAN: Oh. Well. Okay. Thank you.
ZOE: Don't mention it.
EVAN: That's really great news.

(She takes a breath, struggles with how to articulate this.)

ZOE: It's just, The Connor Project . . . I mean, it's great. But maybe we don't have to talk about my brother all the time. Maybe we can talk about . . . other things.
EVAN: I just thought maybe you'd want to know.
ZOE: No, I know you did, but it's just . . . my whole life, everything has always been about Connor. And right now, I just want . . . I need something just for me. If this is going to be a . . .

(She chooses the word carefully.)

. . . relationship, I don't want it to be about my brother. Or the orchard. Or the emails. I just want . . . I want you.

ONLY US

ZOE:

I don't need you to sell me on reasons to want you
I don't need you to search for the proof that I should
You don't have to convince me

You don't have to be scared you're not enough
'Cause what we've got going is good

I don't need more reminders of all that's been broken
I don't need you to fix what I'd rather forget
Clear the slate and start over
Try to quiet the noises in your head
We can't compete with all that

So, what if it's us?
What if it's us and only us?
And what came before
Won't count anymore, or matter
Can we try that?

What if it's you?
And what if it's me?
And what if that's all that we need it to be?
And the rest of the world falls away
What do you say?

EVAN:

I never thought there'd be someone like you
Who would want me

ZOE *(Laughs)*: Well . . .

EVAN:

So I give you ten thousand reasons to not let me go
But if you really see me
If you like me for me and nothing else
Well, that's all that I've wanted
For longer than you could possibly know

EVAN *(con't)*:

> *So it can be us*
> *It can be us and only us*
> *And what came before*
> *Won't count anymore or matter*
> *We can try that*

EVAN/ZOE:

> *It's not so impossible*

EVAN:

> *Nobody else but the two of us here*

EVAN/ZOE:

> *'Cause you're saying it's possible*

ZOE:

> *We can just watch the whole world disappear*

EVAN/ZOE:

> *'Til you're the only one I still know how to see*

EVAN:

> *It's just you and me*

ZOE:

> *It'll be us*
> *It'll be us and only us*
> *And what came before*
> *Won't count anymore*

EVAN/ZOE:

> *We can try that*

You and me
That's all that we need it to be
And the rest of the world falls away
And the rest of the world falls away
The world falls away
The world falls away
And it's only us

FIVE

School.
   Evan runs right into Alana.

ALANA: Where were you last night?

   (Evan looks at her, confused.)

   I waited in the senior parking lot for twenty-three minutes.
EVAN *(Remembering)*: Oh, shit. I completely forgot.
ALANA: Don't worry, I went downtown and handed out the
   postcards without you.
EVAN: I'm really sorry. I must have put the wrong date in my
   phone . . .
ALANA: What is your deal, Evan? The Kickstarter deadline is a
   week from now and I feel like you are just like a thousand

miles away. You haven't made any new videos. You haven't posted on the blog in like forever . . .

EVAN: Well, I was . . . I've been busy.

ALANA: Busy with what?

EVAN: Just . . . different stuff. How much money do we have left to raise?

ALANA: Oh. Not much. Just seventeen thousand dollars.

EVAN: I'm sure we'll get there. We just need to, you know, keep people engaged.

ALANA: Exactly. That's why I'm putting the emails between you and Connor online.

(Evan's stomach drops.)

EVAN: What do you mean?

ALANA: Mrs. Murphy sent them to me. She said, there are a ton more, too. That you, like, show her a new one every week.

EVAN: Well, but they're not, those conversations are really, they're private.

(Alana doesn't understand what he's talking about.)

ALANA: Um, not anymore. They belong to everyone now. I mean, that's the whole point. The more private they are, the better. That's what people want to see. We have a responsibility to our community to show them everything, to tell them the truth.

EVAN: Our "community"?

ALANA: I'm sending you a list of questions to answer, because some of the emails don't make sense.

EVAN: What?

ALANA: Well, like, you've been telling everyone that the first time you went to the orchard was the day you broke your arm. But then in other emails, you talk about going there together since, like, last November . . .

EVAN: Well, that's because, I mean, those are probably just typos, and it sounds like you're reading into them, like, way too much . . .

ALANA: You can explain it all when I send you the questions. You know how much the community loves hearing from you.

(Alana exits as Jared enters.)

JARED: Hey, so my parents are out of town this weekend. The last time they used the liquor cabinet was, like, Rosh Hashanah 1997, so we can drink whatever we want.

EVAN: I can't this weekend. I have seventeen thousand dollars to raise. Remember The Connor Project? You're supposed to be working on this?

JARED: Uh, remember you told me you didn't need my help?

EVAN: I didn't tell you to do nothing. I know you think this is all a joke but it isn't. It's important.

JARED: For Connor.

EVAN: Yeah.

JARED: You know, when you really stop and think about it, Connor being dead, that's pretty much the best thing that's ever happened to you, isn't it?

EVAN: That's a horrible thing to say.

JARED: Well, but, no, think about it. If Connor hadn't died, no one would even know who you are. I mean, people at school actually *talk* to you now. You're almost . . . *popular*. Which is just . . . wonder of wonders, miracle of miracles.

EVAN: I don't care about any of that. I don't care if people at school know who I am. All I wanted was to / help the Murphys.

JARED: / Help the Murphys. Yeah. I know. You keep saying that.

(Zoe enters.)

ZOE: Hey Jared. *(To Evan)* Hi.

(She kisses Evan and takes his hand, a public announcement of their relationship.)

JARED: Look at you, helping the Murphys.

(Jared exits.)

ZOE *(To Evan)*: What was that?
EVAN *(Hiding his misgivings with a smile)*: It's nothing.

SIX

The Murphys' living room.
    Larry pours wine for himself, Cynthia, and Heidi.

CYNTHIA *(To Heidi)*: Evan tells us you're studying to be a lawyer?
HEIDI: Paralegal.
CYNTHIA *(Looking to Larry)*: You're kidding.
LARRY: I had no idea.
CYNTHIA: Aren't you / —they're always looking for paralegals.
LARRY: / We're always, my firm, we're literally *always* trying to find new paralegals.
HEIDI: I have another year to go before I even . . .
LARRY: Well, why don't I give you my card at least . . .

(He reaches into his wallet.)

. . . and when you graduate, / you should absolutely . . .

CYNTHIA: / That is a great idea. Kismet.

HEIDI: Oh. No. You don't have to do that.

CYNTHIA: It's kismet.

(Uncomfortable, Heidi has no choice but to accept the card.)

HEIDI: Well. Thank you.

LARRY: Is red okay, Heidi?

HEIDI: Red would be great.

CYNTHIA: It's from a vineyard outside of Portland—completely one hundred percent sustainable, the entire production process. They had a whole feature on them in the *New York Times.* Incredible.

LARRY: Not to mention, it tastes good, too.

(Larry passes out the wine glasses.)

Cheers.

(They drink.)

HEIDI: I'm so glad that you called this morning. I was, I've been agonizing over whether I should, if it was appropriate for me to reach out . . .

CYNTHIA: Oh, Heidi. We have, too. Evan says you're so busy, I didn't know if I should bother you . . .

HEIDI: I'm not that busy.

CYNTHIA: Well, I asked Evan if you minded him spending so much time here and he said it wasn't a problem because of your schedule. With classes and work . . .

HEIDI: He . . . spends so much time here?

LARRY: Evan's been a real . . . he's been a great source of comfort for us these past few months.

CYNTHIA: Well, he and Connor, they were very close.

HEIDI: I have to admit, I didn't . . . I really had no idea that he and Connor were even . . .

LARRY: We were the same.

CYNTHIA: Boys love to keep secrets.

LARRY: We'd never heard about Evan, we'd never met him . . .

HEIDI: Evan didn't tell me anything.

CYNTHIA: Secret handshakes, secret tree houses . . .

(The front door opens and Zoe and Evan enter.)

ZOE: Sorry we're late. Band went long again.

CYNTHIA: We're just in here having a glass of wine, getting to know each other.

(Evan stops cold when he sees his mother.)

LARRY: We invited your mom to come join us for dinner tonight.

EVAN: Oh.

HEIDI: I didn't realize that Evan was, that you were joining us, too.

CYNTHIA: I'm sorry, I didn't think to tell you.

ZOE *(Shaking hands)*: Hi, I'm Zoe. It's so nice to meet you. Finally.

HEIDI *(Puzzled)*: Oh. Good.

EVAN *(To Zoe)*: Did you know about this?

ZOE: It was my idea.

LARRY: Why don't you guys come sit down?

(Evan and Zoe do.)

EVAN *(To Heidi)*: I thought you had work tonight.

HEIDI: Well, this seemed more important. So. I'm playing hooky.

CYNTHIA: We were just talking about how sneaky you and Connor were. Top secret.

EVAN (*Changing the subject*): Something smells good.

CYNTHIA: Chicken Milanese . . .

HEIDI: I didn't realize you were spending so much time here.

EVAN: You've been working a lot.

HEIDI: Why did I think you were at Jared's?

EVAN: I don't know.

CYNTHIA: Oh but Evan, you call and tell your mother when you're staying the night, right?

EVAN (*Looking away from Heidi*): Of course.

LARRY: You can rest assured we take very good care of him. We've got, he has a toothbrush, so we're not sending him to bed with cavities.

HEIDI: How nice.

ZOE (*To Heidi*): Evan was showing me all of those scholarship contests that you found. That was really impressive. There are, like, a million.

HEIDI: Well, Evan is a great writer.

LARRY: I don't find that hard to believe at all.

HEIDI: His teacher last year for English said he wrote one of the best papers she'd ever read about *Sulu*.

CYNTHIA: How about that.

EVAN (*Quietly*): It's *Sula*.

HEIDI: What did I say?

EVAN: Sulu.

HEIDI: Okay.

LARRY: Sulu is a character on *Star Trek*, I believe . . .

(*Everyone laughs, except for Heidi and Evan.*)

HEIDI: My mistake.

(*Zoe looks at her parents.*)

ZOE: Speaking of scholarships . . .

(Evan looks at Zoe, confused.)

LARRY: I guess now is as good a time as any. Cynthia, do you want to . . . ?

CYNTHIA: Well. Zoe happened to mention to us the other day that Evan was having some difficulty in terms of . . . the financial burdens of college. And Larry and I started thinking about it. And we were very fortunate to have been able to set aside some money for our son . . .

(Cynthia begins to falter, emotion creeping into her voice.
Larry takes her hand.
She waves him away, smiling stoically.)

I'm okay. I'm okay.

(She takes a breath.)

I called you this morning to invite you to come join us for dinner tonight, Heidi, because . . . well, first of all, because we want to thank you for allowing your son to have come into our lives. He was a dear, dear friend to our Connor, and we have come to just love him to pieces.

(Larry and Zoe laugh.)

And with your blessing, we would like to give Evan the money we put away for our son so that he can use it to fulfill his dreams, just like he helped Connor . . .

(She struggles to finish the thought.)

. . . fulfill his.

(A terrible silence.
Heidi is stunned.
Evan feels like puking.
Larry, Cynthia, and Zoe look at them expectantly, hopefully.)

LARRY: What do you think?

(Beat.
Heidi manages to plaster on a stiff smile.)

HEIDI: Wow. I'm, that is . . . I don't know what to say. I'm . . .
LARRY: It would be such a gift to us if we could do this for Evan.
CYNTHIA: It would be a tremendous gift, Heidi.
HEIDI: Well, thank you so much, but . . . we're going to be fine.
      I don't have a lot of money, but I do have some.
CYNTHIA: Oh we didn't mean / at all—
HEIDI: / No, no, I understand, I'm just, we do have money.
      So I'm sorry that you were under the impression that we
      didn't. And, whatever money we don't have, Evan will
      either get a scholarship or he'll go to a community col-
      lege and that's . . . I think that's the best thing for us to do.
      I don't want Evan to get the idea that it's okay to rely on
      other people for favors.
LARRY: It's not a favor.
HEIDI: Well, but, as his mother, I need to set that example for
      him. That you can't expect things from strangers.
CYNTHIA: We are not strangers.
HEIDI: No. Of course not.

(Heidi stands.)

      Thank you for the wine. It was delicious.
CYNTHIA: You're not staying for dinner?
HEIDI: I think I'd better go to work after all.

CYNTHIA: Oh no.

HEIDI: If I'd known Evan was so concerned about our finances, I would never taken the night off in the first place.

(Heidi goes, leaving the Murphys and Evan sitting there, silent.)

SEVEN

The Hansens' house. Living room.

HEIDI: Do you have any idea how *mortifying* it is? To find out that your son has been spending every night in somebody else's home and you didn't even *know* it? You told me you were at Jared's.

EVAN: If you're not here, then why does it matter where I am?

HEIDI: They think you're their son. These people.

EVAN: They're not "these people." They're my . . .

HEIDI: What? / What are they?

EVAN: / I don't know.

HEIDI: Because they act like you're their, like they've adopted you, like I'm just, like I don't even exist.

EVAN: They take care of me.

HEIDI: They're not your parents. That is not your family, Evan.

EVAN: They're nice to me.

HEIDI: Oh they're lovely, lovely people.

EVAN: Yep.

HEIDI: They don't know you.

EVAN: And you do?

HEIDI: I thought I did.

EVAN: What do you know about me? You don't know anything about me. You never even see me.

HEIDI: I am trying my best.

EVAN: They like me. I know how hard that is to believe. They don't think that I'm, that there's something wrong with me, that I need to be fixed, like you do.

HEIDI: When have I *ever* said that?

EVAN: I have to go to therapy, I have to take drugs.

HEIDI: I'm your mother. My job is to take care of you.

EVAN: I know. I'm such a burden. I'm the worst thing that ever happened to you. I ruined your life.

HEIDI: You are the only . . . the one good thing that has *ever* happened to me, Evan.

(Beat.)

I'm sorry I can't give you anything more than that. Shit.

EVAN: Well, it's not my fault that other people can.

(He leaves.
Heidi stands there, stunned.)

GOOD FOR YOU

HEIDI:

> *So you found a place where the grass is greener*
> *And you jumped the fence to the other side*
> *Is it good?*
> *Are they giving you a world I could never provide?*

Well I hope you're proud of your big decision
Yeah I hope it's all that you want and more
Now you're free
From the agonizing life you were living before

And you say what you need to say
So that you get to walk away
It would kill you to have to stay
Trapped when you've got somethin' new
Well I'm sorry you had it rough
And I'm sorry I'm not enough
Thank God they rescued you

So you got what you always wanted
So you got your dream-come-true
Well, good for you
Good for you you
You got a taste of a life so perfect
So you did what you had to do
Good for you
Good for you

(School.
Alana storms up to Evan.)

ALANA: Why did Connor kill himself?

EVAN *(Taken aback)*: Wait what?

ALANA: He was doing better. That's what he told you. In every single email. And then a month later, he kills himself? Why do so many things in these emails just not make sense?

EVAN: Because sometimes things *don't* make sense, okay? Things are messy and complicated . . .

ALANA: Like you dating Zoe? *(Lowering her voice)* Do you know what people are saying about you?

EVAN: Why are you so obsessed with this? I mean, you didn't even know him.

ALANA: Because it's important.

EVAN: Because you were lab partners? Or because, I don't know, maybe because you want another extracurricular for your college applications?

ALANA: Because I know what it's like to feel invisible. Just like Connor. To feel invisible and alone and like nobody would even notice if you vanished into thin air. I bet you used to know what that felt like, too.

(As Alana goes, Jared enters.)

EVAN *(To Jared)*: We need more emails. Emails showing that he was getting worse.

(Jared scoffs.)

This isn't funny.

JARED: Oh I think it's hilarious. I think everyone would probably think it's hilarious.

EVAN: What is that supposed to mean?

JARED: It means, you should remember who your friends are.

EVAN: I thought the only reason you even talk to me is because of your car insurance.

JARED: So?

EVAN: So maybe the only reason you talk to me, Jared, is because you don't have any other friends.

JARED: I could tell everyone everything.

EVAN: Go ahead. Do it. Tell everyone how you helped write emails pretending to be a kid who killed himself.

JARED *(Like a helpless, heartbroken little kid)*: Fuck you, Evan. Asshole.

(He turns and goes.
Evan stands there, assaulted from all directions, unable to escape.)

ALANA:

> Does it cross your mind to be slightly sorry?
> Do you even care that you might be wrong?
> Was it fun?
> Well I hope you had a blast
> While you dragged me along

JARED:

> And you say what you need to say
> And you play who you need to play
> And if somebody's in your way
> Crush them and leave them behind

JARED/ALANA:

> Well, I guess if I'm not of use
> Go ahead, you can cut me loose
> Go ahead now, I won't mind

HEIDI:

> I'll shut my mouth and I'll let you go
> Is that good for you?
> Would that be good for you, you, you?

ALANA/HEIDI:

> I'll just sit back while you run the show
> Is that good for you?
> Would that be good for you, you, you?

ALANA/HEIDI/JARED: EVAN:

> I'll shut my mouth   All I need is some time
> And I'll let you go   To think
> Is that good for you?   But the boat

137

ALANA/HEIDI/JARED *(con't)*:
> *Would that be*
> *Good for you, you, you?*

> *I'll just sit back*
> *While you run the show*
> *Is that good for you?*
> *Good for you?*

> *So you got what you always wanted*
> *So you got your dream come true*

EVAN/ALANA/JARED/HEIDI:
> *Good for you*
> *Good for you you*
> *You got a taste of a life so perfect*
> *Now you say that you're someone*
>> *new*
> *Good for you*
> *Good for you*
> *Good for you*
> *Good for you*

ALANA/JARED/HEIDI:
> *So you got what you always*
>> *wanted*

EVAN *(con't)*:
> *Is about to sink*
> *Can't erase*
> *What I wrote in ink*
> *Tell me how can I change*
> *The story?*

> *All the words that I*
> *Can't take back*
> *Like a train comin'*
> *Off the track*
> *As the rails and the bolts*
> *All crack*
> *I gotta find a way to*
> *Stop it stop it*
> *Just let me out*

EIGHT

Evan, alone.

EVAN: I'm not doing this. I'm done.
CONNOR: You can't just stop now.

(*And Connor is there.*)

EVAN: I don't think I can live with this anymore.
CONNOR: What about my parents?
EVAN: No more emails.
CONNOR: How can you do this to them?
EVAN: No more Connor Project. No more orchard.
CONNOR: After everything they've done for you? They need you.
EVAN: Need me for what? To keep lying to them?
CONNOR: That lie is the only thing that's keeping them together.
EVAN: That's not true.

CONNOR: Oh really? They seemed like a pretty happy family when you met them?

EVAN: I don't want to lie anymore.

CONNOR: And what about Zoe?

EVAN: Zoe said, she just . . . she wants me.

CONNOR: Right.

EVAN: She likes me for who I am.

CONNOR: Except you didn't happen to mention that everything you've told her, it's all been one big fucking lie, did you?

(Evan says nothing.)

Oh. You left that part out.

EVAN: So then, what if . . . what if I did tell her the truth?

CONNOR: She'll hate you.

EVAN: Maybe she would understand. Maybe everyone would understand.

CONNOR: Everyone will hate you.

EVAN: Not if I can just, if I can explain it, you know?

CONNOR: You'll go right back to where you started. No friends.

EVAN: I want to be done / with this.

CONNOR: / Nobody. Nothing. Alone.

EVAN: I'm ready to be done with it.

CONNOR: If you really believe that, then why are you standing here, talking to yourself? Again?

(Pause.)

You think you're going to turn around all of a sudden and start telling everyone the truth? You can't even tell yourself the truth.

EVAN: What are you talking about?

CONNOR: How did you break your arm?

(A pall comes over Evan.)

How did you break your arm, Evan?

EVAN: I fell.

CONNOR: Really? Is that what happened?

EVAN *(Less and less confident)*: I was, I lost my grip and I . . . I fell.

CONNOR: Did you fall? Or did you let go?

(Silence.)

You can get rid of me whenever you want. You can get rid of all of it. The Connor Project. The orchard. But then all that you're going to be left with is . . . you.

FOR FOREVER (REPRISE)

CONNOR:

> *End of May or early June*
> *This picture-perfect afternoon we share*
> *Drive the winding country road*
> *Grab a scoop at "À La Mode"*
> *And then we're there . . .*

Think about it.

(Evan stands there for a moment, lost.
He makes a decision.
Lights shift and Evan and Alana are in their bedrooms, online.
Connor is gone.)

EVAN: I've been a bad co-president. I know that. And I'm sorry. But I'm, you were right, you were absolutely right, and

I'm back and I'm re-dedicating myself to doing everything I can do to make this work.

ALANA: Too late. I've moved on.

EVAN: You've "moved on"?

ALANA: You've made it abundantly clear to me that you're not very interested in being a part of The Connor Project.

EVAN: I can make more videos. I can write more stuff for the blog.

ALANA: I can do all of that myself.

EVAN: It's not the same. You know it's not the same. People want to hear what I have to say. I was his best friend.

ALANA: You know, frankly, Evan? I'm starting to wonder if that's even true.

*(Evan freezes.
He tries laughing it off.)*

EVAN: What does that mean?

ALANA: You keep saying you were best friends. You're like a broken freaking record about it. But nobody ever saw you together. Nobody knew that you were friends.

EVAN: It was a secret. He didn't want us to talk at / school.

ALANA: / I know the story, Evan. We all know the story. We've all heard it a bazillion times.

EVAN: You've seen the emails.

ALANA: Do you know how easy it is to create a fake email account? Backdate emails? Because I do.

(Evan begins to feel desperate.)

You know what? I don't have time for this. I have to raise seventeen thousand dollars.

EVAN: I can prove it.

ALANA: How?

(Long pause.)

EVAN: Here.

(Evan sends Alana an email.
Alana opens it.
Her eyes widen.
The letter.)

If we weren't friends, then why did he write his suicide note to me?

ALANA: Oh my God.

EVAN: Do you believe me now?

ALANA *(Reading)*: "Dear Evan Hansen:"

EVAN: Nobody else has seen this.

ALANA: "It turns out, this wasn't an amazing day after all. This isn't going to be an amazing week or an amazing year."

EVAN: You can't show it to anyone, okay? Nobody else needs to see it.

ALANA: This is *exactly* what people need to see. We need something to create new interest.

EVAN: Can you just please delete it now?

ALANA: Don't you care about building the orchard? This is the best way to make Connor's dream come true.

EVAN: No, it isn't.

(And the letter is suddenly everywhere, Evan's words filling the screens.
Alana turns away from Evan, speaking now to the world.)

ALANA: Dear Connor Project Community:

(The blood drains from Evan's face, as he realizes what's happened.)

EVAN: You put it online.

(*Alana continues to speak to the online community, ignoring Evan entirely.*)

ALANA: Connor's note is a message to all of us. Share it with as many people as you can. Post it everywhere.

EVAN (*Begging*): You need to take it down. Please.

ALANA: If you've ever felt alone like Connor, then please consider making a donation to The Connor Murphy Memorial Orchard. No amount is too small.

(*Voices from the virtual world begin to pile up on top of each other, stacking and accumulating, accreting.*
Unlike before, the Voices do not fuse—they congeal.
This is not a community, but a hydra-headed herd-thing, primal and ravenous and cruel.)

VOICES:
Have people seen this?

Connor Murphy's suicide note

This is the actual, authentic

Forward

The whole world needs to see this.

Share it with everyone you know

This is why the orchard is so important, guys

I just gave fifty dollars for the orchard and I think everyone else should give as much as they can

Re-post

His parents present themselves

He wrote his suicide note to Evan Hansen, because he knew his family didn't give a shit

His parents, by the way, are insanely rich

YOU WILL BE FOUND (REPRISE)

VOICES:	A/J/VIRTUAL VOICES:
Forward	*Oh*
Share	
Like	
Maybe they should have spent their money on helping their son instead of	*Oh*
Please re-tweet	
Evan Hansen was the only one who was paying any attention	*Oh*
Favorite	
Share	
Forward	
	Oh

(Elsewhere, Zoe appears, reading her own screen, horrified.)

VOICES:
"Like all my hope is pinned on Zoe"

A/J/VV:
Oh

Zoe's a stuck-up bitch, I go to
school with her, trust me

Share

VV:
Oh

Forward

Someone will
Come runnin'

Larry Murphy is a corporate
lawyer who only cares about

Oh

Cynthia Murphy is one of
these disgusting women

Oh

Oh

Oh

ZOE: Mom? You need to see this.

Oh

Someone will
Come runnin'

(Cynthia enters.)

A: J:
Oh

VOICES:
A hundred and sixty more
dollars and the orchard will
be fully funded

Oh

Fuck the Murphys

A/J:
Make them feel what   *You are not alone*
Connor felt

I love you guys

Oh my God, we are two hundred
dollars over our goal

Their house is at the end of the   A/VV/J:
cul-de-sac with the red door   *You are not alone*

(Cynthia reads over Zoe's shoulder.)

Zoe's bedroom window is on the right

The gate to the back is completely unlocked

CYNTHIA: How did they . . . ?

(Larry enters.)   A/VV: J/VV:

VOICES:
Zoe's cell phone number,
if my sources are correct   *You are not*
                                       alone   *You are not*
                                                            alone
I gave twenty
                                   You are not
                                       alone   *You are not*
                                                            alone

CYNTHIA: It's everywhere.

VOICES: A/J/VV:
I'm not saying to do
anything illegal   *You are not*

All hours, day and night

147

voices *(con't):*
A thousand

Ring the doorbell

Keep calling until they answer.

A/J/VV *(con't):*

You are not alone

NINE

Lights snap up on the Murphys' living room.
Larry stares at his cell phone.
Zoe sits, looking at the laptop.
Cynthia paces behind her.
Evan stands, nauseous.

CYNTHIA: Where did they get Connor's note?
LARRY: I don't know.
EVAN: I tried to call Alana, but she's / not answering.
CYNTHIA *(To Larry)*: / Some of these are adults. Do you see
their pictures? These are adults.

(A cell phone rings.
Zoe reaches for it.)

LARRY: Maybe let it ring, Zoe.

ZOE (*Into phone*): Hello?

(*Beat.*
Her face remains impassive.)

LARRY: Who is it? Who is it, / Zoe?
ZOE (*Into phone*): / Have fun with your miserable life. Bye.

(*Zoe hangs up.*)

LARRY: What's the number?
ZOE: It's blocked. Who cares?
CYNTHIA: What did they say to you?
ZOE: It doesn't matter.
LARRY: Did they threaten you?
ZOE: It doesn't matter, Dad.
CYNTHIA: I'm calling the police. That's it.

(*Cynthia digs through her purse for her cell phone.*)

LARRY: Right now, maybe the best thing to do is to just wait and
    see if this blows over.
CYNTHIA: That's always your solution, isn't it? Do nothing.
LARRY: Is that what I said?
ZOE: Can you guys just stop?
CYNTHIA: Wait and see. Let's wait and see, right, Larry?
LARRY: What are the police going to do? It's the internet.
    They're going to arrest the internet?
CYNTHIA: I had to beg you, every step / of the way.
LARRY: / Okay. Hold on.
EVAN (*Quietly*): I really think they're going to stop . . .
CYNTHIA: I had to *plead* with you. For therapy, rehab . . .
LARRY: You went lurching from one miracle cure to the next.
CYNTHIA (*Laughs*): "Miracle cure." / Really. Is that what you call
    it?

LARRY: / Because all he needed was another twenty-thousand-dollar weekend yoga retreat.

EVAN: Maybe I should try calling Alana again . . .

CYNTHIA: And what was your alternative? Other than picking apart everything I did?

LARRY: Putting him on a program and *sticking* to it.

ZOE: No, you wanted to punish him.

CYNTHIA: Listen to your daughter, Larry.

ZOE: You treated him like a criminal.

CYNTHIA *(To Larry)*: Are you listening?

ZOE *(To Cynthia)*: You think you were any better? You let him do whatever he wanted.

LARRY: Thank you.

CYNTHIA *(To Larry)*: When he threatened to kill himself the first time, do you remember what you said?

LARRY: Oh for Christ's sake.

CYNTHIA: "He just wants attention."

LARRY: I'm not going to sit here and defend myself.

CYNTHIA: He was *getting better*. Ask Evan. Tell him, Evan.

(Evan freezes, the unmistakable sensation of his hands clamming up.)

EVAN: I shouldn't, um . . .

CYNTHIA: Evan did everything he could.

LARRY: Evan was in denial of what was happening / right in front of him.

ZOE: / Don't put him in the middle of this.

CYNTHIA *(Going to the computer)*: Read the note, Larry. Read what he said. "I wish that everything was different." / He wanted to be different. He wanted to be better.

LARRY: / I did the best I could, I tried to help him the only way I knew how, and if that's not good enough . . .

EVAN *(Overlapping them)*: No . . . no . . . no . . .

CYNTHIA: He was trying to be better. He was trying.
LARRY: And he was *failing*.
CYNTHIA: *We* failed *him*.

(*Evan can bear it no longer.*)

EVAN: No you didn't.

(*They turn to look at him.*)

You didn't fail him.
CYNTHIA: Look at what he wrote . . .
EVAN: He didn't write it.

(*Long pause.*)

I wrote it.

(*Silence.*)

CYNTHIA (*A ludicrous notion*): You didn't write Connor's suicide
note, Evan.
EVAN: It wasn't a . . . it was an assignment from my therapist.
Write a letter to yourself. A pep talk. "Dear Evan Hansen:
Today is going to be an amazing day and here's why."
LARRY (*Unable to make sense of this*): I don't think . . .
EVAN: I was supposed to bring it to my appointment. Connor
took it from me and I guess he must have had it with him
when you . . . found him.
ZOE: What are you talking about?
EVAN: We weren't friends.
CYNTHIA: No. No no no.

WORDS FAIL

EVAN:

> *I never meant to make it such a mess*
> *I never thought that it would go this far*

CYNTHIA: There were emails. You showed us the emails.

EVAN:

> *So I just stand here*
> *Sorry, searching*
> *For something to say*
> *Something to say*

LARRY: But you knew about the orchard. He took you to the orchard.

CYNTHIA: That's where you broke your arm.

EVAN: I broke my arm at Ellison Park. By myself.

CYNTHIA: No, that day at the orchard, you and Connor at the orchard . . .

EVAN:

> *Words fail*
> *Words fail*
> *There's nothing I can say*

CYNTHIA *(The truth finally beginning to sink in)*: Oh God.

ZOE *(Not easy to say)*: But you told me that he . . . that you would talk about me and that he would . . .

(Beat.)

How could you do this?

EVAN:

I guess . . . I thought I could be part of this
I never had this kind of thing before
I never had that perfect girl who
Somehow could see
The good part of me

I never had the dad who stuck it out
No corny jokes or baseball gloves
No mom who just was there
'Cause mom was all that she had to be

That's not a worthy explanation
I know there is none
Nothing can make sense of all these things I've done

Words fail
Words fail
There's nothing I can say

Except sometimes you see ev'rything you've wanted
And sometimes you see ev'rything you wish you had
And it's right there, right there
Right there in front of you

And you want to believe it's true
So you make it true
And you think
Maybe ev'rybody wants it, needs it a little bit too

(Zoe stands.
She looks at Evan.
She goes.
Cynthia goes after her.

Larry stands there for a moment.
Finally, he, too, goes.
Evan turns to see Connor there.
The light slowly, very slowly goes out on Connor.
And Evan is alone.)

This was just a sad invention
It wasn't real, I know
But we were happy
I guess I couldn't let that go
I guess I couldn't give that up
I guess I wanted to believe
'Cause if I just believe
Then I don't have to see what's really there

No, I'd rather
Pretend I'm something better than these broken parts
Pretend I'm something other than this mess that I am
'Cause then I don't have to look at it
And no one gets to look at it
No, no one can really see
'Cause I've learned to slam on the brake
Before I even turn the key
Before I make the mistake
Before I lead with the worst of me
I never let them see the worst of me

'Cause what if ev'ryone saw?
What if ev'ryone knew?
Would they like what they saw?
Or would they hate it too?
Will I just keep on running away from what's true?

All I ever do is run

EVAN *(con't):*
> *So how do I step in*
> *Step into the sun?*
> *Step into the sun*

(The Hansen living room. Evan enters to find Heidi sitting on the sofa, on her laptop.
She looks up at him.)

HEIDI: Have you seen this? The note that Connor Murphy . . .

(Evan nods.)

It's all over everyone's Facebook.

(Beat.)

"Dear Evan Hansen."

(She looks at him, the words familiar.
Evan says nothing.)

Did you . . . you wrote this? This note?

(Beat.
Evan nods.)

I didn't know.

EVAN: No one did.

HEIDI: No, that's not what I . . . I didn't know that you . . . that you were . . . hurting. Like that. That you felt so . . . I didn't know. How did I not know?

EVAN: Because I never told you.

HEIDI: You shouldn't have had to.

EVAN: I lied. About . . . so many things. Not just Connor. Last summer, I just . . . I felt so alone . . .

(He can't go any further than this.)

HEIDI: You can tell me.

EVAN *(Shakes his head)*: You'll hate me.

HEIDI: Oh, Evan.

EVAN: You should. If you knew what I tried to do. If you knew who I am, how . . . broken I am.

HEIDI: I already know you. And I love you.

(Beat.)

EVAN: I'm so sorry.

HEIDI: I can promise you, some day all of this . . . this will all feel like a very long time ago.

(Evan shrugs, not believing her.)

EVAN: I don't know.

HEIDI: Your dad . . . do you remember the day he drove by to get his things?

(Evan shakes his head.)

It was a few weeks after he moved out. "Temporarily," we said . . .

SO BIG/SO SMALL

HEIDI:

It was a February day
When your dad came by before goin' away
A U-Haul truck in the driveway
The day it was suddenly real

I told you not to come outside
But you saw that truck and you smiled so wide
A real live truck in your driveway
We let you sit behind the wheel

Goodbye, goodbye
Now it's just me and my little guy

And the house felt so big
And I felt so small
The house felt so big
And I felt so small

That night I tucked you into bed
I will never forget how you sat up and said:
"Is there another truck comin' to our driveway
A truck that will take Mommy away?"

And the house felt so big
And I felt so small
The house felt so big
And I . . .

And I knew there would be moments that I'd miss
And I knew there would be space I couldn't fill

And I knew I'd come up short a million diff'rent ways
And I did, and I do, and I will

But like that February day
I will take your hand, squeeze it tightly and say:
"There's not another truck in the driveway
Your mom isn't goin' anywhere
Your mom is stayin' right here"
Your mom isn't goin' anywhere
Your mom is stayin' right here
No matter what
I'll be here . . .

When it all feels so big
'Til it all feels so small
When it all feels so big
'Til it all feels so small
'Til it all feels so small

(Evan goes.
His mother lets him go.)

You'll see. I promise.

(Heidi exits.
Life goes on.
Hearts break and mend and break once more.
Time does its work.
Slowly, the sky begins to open.
It is enormous.
A vast green field.
As far as the eye can see: rows and columns of wooden stakes
planted in the grass.
Tied to each stake, a small, spindly tree.

An orchard.
Zoe, sitting on a wrought iron bench, waits, nervous.
After a moment, Evan enters.)

EVAN: Hey.
ZOE: Hi.

(They smile, a bit awkward.
Beat.)

EVAN: How are you?
ZOE: Good. Pretty good.
EVAN: You graduate soon, right?
ZOE: In two weeks.
EVAN: Wow. How's being a senior?
ZOE: Busy.
EVAN: I remember that.
ZOE: How's being a freshman?
EVAN: Oh. Well. I actually decided to take a year off . . .
ZOE: Oh.
EVAN: Yeah. Try to save some money. Get a job. I've been taking
    classes at the community college. So I'll have some credits
    to transfer in the fall.
ZOE: That's smart.
EVAN: Yeah. We'll see.

(Beat.)

In the meantime, though, I can get you a friends and family discount at Pottery Barn. If you're looking for . . . over-
priced home decor.
ZOE: You know, not at the moment . . .

EVAN: Well, if you change your mind . . . I'm only working there for a few more months, though, so the window of opportunity is closing fast.

(They smile.)

ZOE: I always imagine you and Connor here. Even though, obviously . . .

EVAN: This is my first time. I mean, I've probably driven by it a thousand times. I just, every time I think about getting out of the car, I feel like . . . I don't know. I just . . . like I don't deserve to, I guess.

(Beat.)

It's nice. Peaceful.

ZOE: My parents, they're here all the time. We do picnics, like, every weekend. It's helped them. A lot, actually. Having this.

(Beat.)

EVAN: They never told anyone. About Connor's, about the note. About . . . who really wrote it.

(Zoe nods.)

They didn't have to do that. They could have told everyone. What I did.

ZOE: Everybody needed it for something.

EVAN: That doesn't mean it was okay.

ZOE: It saved my parents.

(Pause.)

EVAN: It's weird. I um . . . over the fall, I found this, um, year-book thing my class made in eighth grade. Most people did, like, collages of their friends. Connor's was a list of his ten favorite books. I've been trying to read all of them.

(Beat.)

I know it's not the same thing as knowing him—it's not, at all, but, I don't know, it's . . .

ZOE: Something.

(Pause.)

It's been . . . hard. It's been a hard year.

EVAN *(For him, as well)*: I know.

(Beat.)

I've been wanting to call you for a long time. I didn't really know what I would say, but then I just . . . I decided to call anyway.

ZOE: I'm happy you did.

(Pause.)

EVAN: I wish we could have met now. Today. For the first time.

ZOE: Me too.

(They look at one another for a long time.)

I should probably . . .

EVAN: Of course.

ZOE: It's just, exams are this week . . .

EVAN: No, totally.

(Zoe begins to go.)

Can I ask you, though? Why did, um, why did you want to meet here?

(A long pause.
Zoe looks around.)

ZOE: I wanted to be sure you saw this.

(A beat, and Zoe goes.
Evan takes in the immensity of all that is around him.
Music begins slowly, softly underneath, as one by one the company begins to enter around him.)

EVAN: Dear Evan Hansen:

Today is going to be a good day and here's why. Because today, no matter what else, today at least . . . you're you. No hiding, no lying. Just . . . you. And that's . . . that's enough.

FINALE

HEIDI/ALANA/JARED:
> *All we see is sky*
> *For forever*
> *We let the world*
> *Pass by for forever*

HEIDI/ALANA/JARED/LARRY/
  CYNTHIA:
> *Feels like we could*
> *Go on for forever*

	HEIDI/ALANA/JARED/LARRY/
	CYNTHIA:
EVAN: Maybe some day, every-	*This way*
thing that happened . . .	
maybe it will all feel like	*This way*
a distant memory.	

Maybe some day no one will even remember about The Connor Project. Or me. Maybe some day, some other kid is going to be standing here, staring out at the trees, feeling so . . . alone, wondering if maybe the world might look different from all the way up there. Better. Maybe he'll start climbing, one branch at a time, and he'll keep going, even when it seems like he can't find another foothold. Even when it feels . . . hopeless. Like everything is telling him to let go. This time, maybe this time, he won't let go. He'll just . . . hold on and he'll keep going.

He'll keep going until he sees the sun.

(People slowly begin to look around, to see one another, to find one another.)

ALL *(Except Evan)*:
> *All we see is light*
> *Watch the sun burn bright*
> *We could be all right for forever this way*
> *All we see is sky for forever*

(Evan steps forward.)

EVAN:

>*All I see is sky for forever.*

>*(A moment.*
>*A suspension.*
>*Black.)*

END

STEVEN LEVENSON is the book writer for *Dear Evan Hansen*. His plays include *If I Forget*, *The Unavoidable Disappearance of Tom Durnin*, *Core Values*, *The Language of Trees*, and *Seven Minutes in Heaven*. A former Artist in Residence at Ars Nova and a member of the Roundabout Leadership Council, he worked as a writer and producer on Showtime's *Masters of Sex*. He is a founding member of Colt Coeur and an alumnus of MCC's Playwrights Coalition and Ars Nova's Play Group. Honors include an Obie Award, three Outer Critics Circle Awards, a Drama Desk nomination, and the Helen Hayes Award. His plays are published by Dramatists Play Service and Playscripts. A graduate of Brown University, he is a member of the Dramatists Guild of America, Inc.

BENJ PASEK & JUSTIN PAUL are the songwriting team behind *Dear Evan Hansen*. They wrote the lyrics for the musical film *La La Land* (Lionsgate), for which they received the Academy Award for Best Original Song for "City of Stars." Previous musicals include *A Christmas Story: The Musical*, *Dogfight*, *James and the Giant Peach*, and *Edges*. Their film projects include the animated feature *Trolls* (DreamWorks), the live-action movie musical *Snow White* (Disney), and *The Greatest Showman* (FOX). Their television songwriting credits include *The Flash*, *Smash*, and *Johnny and the Sprites*. Honors and awards include an Academy Award, a Golden Globe Award, a Tony nomination, an Emmy nomination, the Drama Desk Award, an

Obie Award, the Outer Critics Circle Award, the Lucille Lortel Award, a London *Evening Standard* nomination, and the Jonathan Larson Award. Both are graduates of the University of Michigan Musical Theatre Program and members of the Dramatists Guild of America, Inc.